ALICE IN KANJI LAND

ALICE IN KANJI LAND

漢字の国のアリス
Kanji no Kuni no Arisu

by Cure Dolly

The Sun Daughter Press

Alice in Kanji Land by Cure Dolly

© 2017 Sun Daughter Press

All rights reserved. No part of this publication may be reproduced, stored in a retrieval system, or transmitted, in any form or by any means, without the prior permission of the copyright holder.

Published by Sun Daughter Press
http://sundaughterpress.com

CONTENTS

Introduction: How to Use This Book 9

1. Follow That Rabbit 11
    How Alice Came to Kanji Land

2. Itchy-Knee-San Is a Japanese Count 16
    Kanji: 日, 月, 一, 二, 三, 四, 五
    Concepts: "Free Radicals"; Combining elements
    Free Radicals: 儿

3. The Rad Hatter 22
    Kanji: 八, 六, 七, 九, 十
    Free Radicals: 亠

4. The Tower of the Ancients 26
    Kanji: 白, 百, 千, 火, 人, 水, 木, 金, 王, 土
    Concepts: Adjective formation; "Glue-names" (*on-yomi*)

5. The Five Ways and Ten Thousand Things 35
    Kanji: 上, 万, 下, 右, 左, 友, 工, 口, 中
    Concepts: Japanese directional expressions

6. The Middle Way 44
    Kanji: 大, 小, 入, 出, 山, 田, 力, 男, 女
    Concepts: Two-kanji word-building; "Ten-ten hooking" (*rendaku*); Class-marking *no*

7. The Child with Six Fingers ………………...…..………… 55
   Kanji: 子, 目, 手, 耳, 足, 止

8. Kin-Kon-KAN-Kon ………………………………………… 61
   Kanji: 赤, 刀, 青, 生, 学, 父, 母, 校, 先, 年
   Free Radicals: 丷, 冖
   Concepts: Three-kanji word-building; "Small-tsu hooking"

9. Down by the Riverside ……………………………………... 75
   Kanji: 川, 花, 化, 雨, 石, 貝, 林, 森
   Free Radicals: 艹, イ, 匕
   Concepts: Same-element combinations

10. The Owl That Went *Pfam!* ……………………………… 85
    Kanji: 休, 見, 立, 天, 気, 气, 本, 犬, 虫, 早, 草

11. The Car That Drove Herself ……………………………… 98
    Kanji: 車, 来, 米, 夕, 名, 前, 正, 音, 竹, 村, 空, 町
    Free Radicals: 刂, 宀

12. The Doll at the Crossroads …..………………………… 111
    Kanji: 円, 糸, 文, 字, 玉

Interlude: With Great Power…

13. The Man Behind the Hats ……………………………… 118
    Kanji: 食, 良, 飲, 長, 間
    Free Radicals: 亠

14. The Time Machine 125
    Kanji: 分, 時, 寺, 週, 周, 半

    Free Radicals: 冂, 辶

    Concepts: Japanese time-expressions; Effects of kana on kanji pronunciation

15. Relativity 135
    Kanji: 今, 午, 後

    Free Radicals: 幺, 彳, 夂

    Concepts: Relative time-expressions

16. Inside the Treasure Cave 143
    Kanji: 行, 聞, 外, 北, 南, 東, 西, 何, 可

    Free Radicals: 卜

17. The Road to Nowhere 152
    Kanji: 道, 自, 首, 店, 占, 売, 士, 買

    Free Radicals: 广, 罒

    Concepts: Japanese "one-word phrases"

18. No-Tea with the Baron 162
    Kanji: 言, 舌, 話, 語, 書, 雷, 電, 駅, 馬, 会

    Free Radicals: 聿, 厶

    Concepts: Sound Sisters

19. The Train of Events 174
    Kanji: 高, 魚, 新, 古, 多, 少, 社, 安

    Free Radicals: 灬, 斤, 礻

20. Was It a Dream? 185
   Kanji: 毎, 国
   Free Radicals: 囗

Afterword

   How to Use the Alice in Kanji Land SRS Deck 191

   Professor Isseki's Geeky Notes 197

   Glossary of Japanese Words 199

Introduction

How to Use This Book

Alice in Kanji Land is primarily intended for two kinds of reader.

1. The new kanji-learner, adult or child

This book will teach all the Japanese school first-year kanji plus all the additional kanji needed for the JLPT N5 exam. It will give you a solid foundation of the most basic kanji, their structure, meanings, and main pronunciations. You will also learn quite a lot of vocabulary and many of the basic concepts of Japanese words.

The book, together with the associated free Anki deck, is a complete course if you want it to be. It not only teaches the first-year and JLPT N5 kanji in the context of real words, not just as "raw kanji", but also shows you how they are built and how they go on to build other words.

If you just want to enjoy the story and pick up some kanji as you go along—as well as the *idea* of how kanji work—that's fine too. In fact, this is a third kind of reader who can benefit from the book—the "kanji-taster" who just wants to get the feel of kanji and of Japanese in general. This is not unimportant because we all went through this stage before deciding to jump in, and having good, assimilable information is crucial.

If you want to use the book to learn the kanji, I recommend using the *Alice in Kanji Land* Anki deck. It is free and you'll find the link in the Afterword at the end of this book. A few minutes each day with this will fix the kanji firmly in your long-term memory by a scientific method that adapts to your personal learning. The app you need to run it is free too, and I explain how to set it up and use it in the Afterword (it's not difficult).

2. The kanji consolidator

The second type of reader is the person who already knows some kanji—maybe quite a lot—but has learned them primarily by "facial recognition", so that she is not quite sure how they are all made up. There is nothing wrong with learning this way, but it can make life increasingly difficult as we go along learning more and more. At some point we need to go back and firm up our understanding right from the beginning kanji.

I did the same myself, and this book partly came out of the techniques I used to consolidate my own kanji, as well as my experiences in helping new learners.

Alice's friends sometimes introduce something that might look like a "grammar point". In fact the line between "grammar" and "vocabulary" is somewhat arbitrary. To give an example, if someone tells you (and they do) that *shita* means under or down, you naturally assume that *shita* is a preposition, like "under" or "down". But it isn't. It is a noun, like "left" or "right", and works the same way they do. So by learning how Japanese directional expressions *work*, we are learning what the words actually *mean*.

Since nobody likes long introductions and everybody wants to meet Alice, I won't say any more here. If you want to learn more about the philosophy behind this book and other introduction-y things, you will need to go to the Afterword at the end.

Things are sometimes topsy-turvy in Kanji Land as you and Alice are about to discover…

1

Follow That Rabbit

Once upon a time there was a girl called Alice. But if you call her Alice she will not answer you, because she likes to be called Arisu.

Now actually there is no difference between Alice and Arisu. Arisu is just Alice said the Japanese way. But you'd better get used to saying Arisu if you want to talk to Alice—I mean, to Arisu. Otherwise she won't answer you.

You see, Arisu likes Japanese things. Even though she is only eight, she has learned to write in Japanese. She can write her name like this:

So, when she finished learning all the Japanese letters, someone told her that there were even more to learn.

Arisu was a bit taken aback by knowing there was a whole 'nother set of letters, though it is really just the same as English.

ABCD is not the same as *abcd*, after all.

So Arisu shouted *ganbaru yo!* And in a few days she could write her name like this:

"So now I'm done with learning letters," said Arisu. "Now I want to go to Japan and have adventures with all the Magical Girls and Hello Kitties."

But a Boring Person appeared. Just like a wild Pokemon really. Boring Persons appear all the time. Like Rattatas. I expect they appear every day where you live too.

And the Boring Person said, "You can't get to Japan from here. And even if you did, you wouldn't have adventures, because there are no Magical Girls or Hello Kitties in Real Japan."

And Arisu said, "I don't believe you! I know all my Japanese letters now and I'm going to Japan."

Arisu put on her walking shoes and started walking. But the Boring Person said, "No matter how far you walk, you'll never get to Japan."

And Arisu said, "Just watch me."

And the Boring Person said, "Now listen to me, Alice…"

But Arisu didn't listen to another word, because the Boring Person had said the Forbidden Word. And once you say that, Arisu can't hear another word you say.

The Boring Person shouted, "You haven't even learned your Japanese letters yet. There are hundreds more! Hundreds and thousands! You'll never do it! You'll never learn them all. And you'll never have adventures because there are no adventures in this world…"

Arisu didn't say anything. She just kept on walking. Somehow she heard everything the Boring Person said, but she pretended not to. She just kept on walking to Japan. But there were tears running down her cheeks.

The Boring Person thought Arisu couldn't hear because she just kept walking and said nothing.

"Alice, listen to me!" shouted the Boring Person.

But Arisu just kept walking toward Japan. Or at any rate in the direction she thought must be toward Japan. Which is east, I think. Or is it west from here?

Then the Boring Person got really angry and threw something at Arisu. It didn't hit her though. It just lay on the ground in front of her. It was a book called

2,136 Joyo Kanji

FOLLOW THAT RABBIT

Arisu looked at the title as she walked past. She wanted to pick the book up, but she didn't want to show that she had heard or seen anything done by a person who called her Alice. So she didn't. She just kept walking to Japan.

The Boring Person followed her shouting things, but Arisu just kept counting from one to ten in Japanese so she couldn't hear what was being said. She wondered how to count up to 2,136. Were there really that many letters in Japanese? Did she have to learn them all before she went to Japan? Would she ever have adventures?

In the end the Boring Person gave up. And Arisu shouted:

"*Yatta!*

"*Ganbatta!*

"*Katta!*"

which she thought meant "I did it! I tried hard! I won!" And so it did.

But by this time she was very tired and kind of cried out, because she had been crying all the time. But the Boring Person didn't know that, so

BE~DA! to the Boring Person.

Arisu pulled down her lower eyelid and stuck out her tongue just to show what she thought about Boring People.

Then she sat down under a tree and wanted to cry some more, but she couldn't because she was cried out.

So she went to sleep.

The last thing she thought before she went to sleep was, "I wish I'd picked up that book. But then the Boring Person would have known I was listening. Are there really 2,136 letters? Are there really no adventures? Should I go back to find the book? Should I keep walking to Japan?

"Japan... Adventures.... Will I ever..... That book....... zzzzz........"

But it was all right about the book because it had followed her. It ran up on its little booky legs and snuggled up beside her. I wonder what the Boring Person would have thought about that. But of course Boring Persons can't see that kind of thing.

So Arisu slept under the tree with the book snuggled against her until she heard a voice calling her. It didn't call her Arisu, but it didn't call her Alice either, so she opened her eyes.

"*Ojou-chan!*" said the voice.

Arisu rubbed her eyes and looked in the direction of the voice. She saw just what you thought she was going to see. A White Rabbit wearing a neat black waistcoat and a stovepipe hat, holding a pocket watch in its hand.

"*Osoku narimashita,*" said the White Rabbit.

"You're... late?" said Arisu, who knew that little bit of Japanese. And then added "*desu*" to be polite. And "*Usagi-san*" to be politer.

"Yes, extremely late," said the White Rabbit. It wasn't talking English. Maybe it was Japanese. Maybe *Usagigo* (Rabbit language). Whatever it was, Arisu could understand it easily.

"*Sumimasen,*" said Arisu. "Am I blocking the way to your hole?"

"Hole?" said the White Rabbit. "What hole? It's the Book I need to go into."

"*Hon?*" said Arisu. She hadn't noticed the book. But there it was. The kanji book the Boring Person had thrown at her. How did that get here? She picked it up.

"Open it please, *ojou-chan,*" said the White Rabbit impatiently.

Arisu opened the book. Immediately the White Rabbit jumped up and landed on the book's open pages. At least, it looked as if it was about to land, but it didn't. It disappeared down the book as if the book had been a hole.

Arisu heard the White Rabbit's voice fading into the distance. It was shouting, "And whatever you do, don't follow me. *Dame, dame.*"

"Well, how *would* I follow anyway?" said Arisu to herself. "Maybe if I poked my head right into the pages as if it were a hole and not a book..."

Arisu tried that, and the world seemed to spin around her. She had the sensation of falling down and down. But gently falling, like a *sakura* petal.

She fell down and down until she landed softly on what felt like grass.

"I suppose I must still be asleep," she said. "If I open my eyes, I'll see the tree and the grass and the sun and the book—the book—is that really here? Or was that part of the dream?"

FOLLOW THAT RABBIT

She opened her eyes. And sure enough there was no book. And there was the tree and the grass and the sun.

The only thing was that the tree looked rather like this:

And the sun... well, the sun looked much squarer than usual. It shone as brightly and happily as ever, but it looked like this:

"How curious," said Arisu. "Wherever can I be?"

2

Itchy-Knee-San Is a Japanese Count

"How curious," said Arisu. "Wherever can I be?"

"Well, that's a question, isn't it?" said someone from behind her.

Arisu turned around to see the White Rabbit. But this time the White Rabbit was dressed in a kimono.

"You changed your clothes," said Arisu.

"Changed my clothes?" said the White Rabbit. "Into what? Cabbage leaves? Of course I haven't changed my clothes. They're still clothes, aren't they?"

"But you were wearing a waistcoat with a gold watch-chain and a stovepipe hat."

The White Rabbit laughed. "Oh, that would be *Oniichan*—my brother Meiji. *Atashi wa Anji desu.*" Anji gave a little bow.

"*Hajimemashite, Anji-san. Yoroshiku onegaishimasu,*" said Arisu, bowing slowly and carefully. Then she said, "Would you mind telling me where I am?"

She said that part in—well, it might have been English or it might not. She didn't know very much Japanese, but she had an idea that she might possibly be speaking and understanding something that was at least half way to Japanese.

"*Ee-to… doko, doko, doko,*" mused Anji. "How do I explain this? You aren't in Kansas any more."

"I never was in Kansas," said Arisu.

"Really? Then you aren't Doroshii-chan?"

"No, that's quite another story. My name is Arisu."

"*Sou desu ka.* Well, this is Kanji Land."

"Kanji—you mean those other letters."

"Letters?" said Anji indignantly. "Kanji aren't letters. They are pictures. They are ideas. They are dreams. They are *adventures.*"

"*Adventures,*" repeated Arisu. "Then they do exist."

"Whoever said they didn't?"

"No one that matters. So why is the sun like that? I mean, square and not round?"

"Well, that's about as round as things get around here. Round things get squared off. That way you can fit every adventure in a square when you're writing. You've seen the symbol for the sun that looks like this, I suppose."

"Yes," said Arisu.

"Well, the kanji is just the same...

...except that the circle is square and the dot has turned into a line. We call the sun *Hi*. Or if you want to be polite (and you should be polite) *o-Hi-sama*."

"I always think of the sun as she, not he, with a big happy smiley face."

"*Hi* might be a she for anything I know, but her name is still *Hi*."

"Is the moon square too?"

"Yes. She looks just like the sun. Except that she has long hair that hangs down from her face. That's why her light seems less bright. Her long hair stops all her rays coming down to us."

"That's not what I learned in school."

"Well, things are probably different in Kansas."

"I've never been to Kansas, so I shouldn't know."

"Of course. I forgot. Her name is *Tsuki*. Isn't that a pretty name? *O-Tsuki-sama*. And the thing is..."

Arisu never found out what the thing was, because at that moment lots of small kanji came running up to see the newcomer. They stared at Arisu and whispered loudly to each other.

"She's rather *round*, isn't she?" said one.

"She seems to have an awful lot of radicals," said another.

"No personal remarks, please," said Anji severely. "Now step up properly and introduce yourselves."

"*Ha~i*," they chimed.

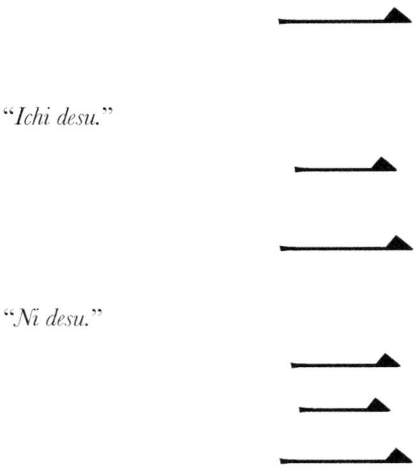

"*Ichi desu.*"

"*Ni desu.*"

"*San desu.*"

"You can just call them Itchy-knee-san. They're always together," said one of the others and burst out laughing.

"Why, they're like the Roman numbers I, II and III laid on their sides," exclaimed Arisu.

"Now who's making personal remarks?" said *Ichi*.

"You mean Roman numbers are like us, stuck upright in the ground like sticks," said *Ni*.

"*Gomen nasai,*" said Arisu, bowing and turning a little pink. She hoped something would happen to distract them from being annoyed with her, and it did.

Suddenly a pair of human-like legs came running past.

儿

"Quick, catch them and put them back in their box," said Anji. *Ichi*, *Ni* and *San* ran after the lively legs.

"Legs?" said Arisu. "Without a body?"

"They are a Free Radical, you see," explained Anji.

"I am afraid I don't see," said Arisu.

"Radicals are *parts* of kanji. These legs don't make a kanji on their own, only when they are part of another kanji. So when they run off like this, we call them Free Radicals. We have to catch them quickly and put them back in their proper place."

"Don't they mind?"

"Oh no. They're lost, you see. Outside of a larger kanji they can't do anything. Except run around blindly. Some kanji can act as radicals but they are still complete by themselves. But Free Radicals are just lost without a bigger kanji to be part of."

"*Sou desu ka...*" said Arisu a little confusedly.

Anji smiled. "For example, *o-Hi-sama* and *o-Tsuki-sama* can be radicals. They can even get together and make another kanji between themselves. Like this:

This one means light. Of course, it would, wouldn't it? The Two Great Lights together. What could it mean but light? You don't need to learn this one yet. It is just to show you how it works.

"*Hi* and *Tsuki* are radicals in this kanji, but if you take them out of it, they aren't lost, are they? They are *o-Hi-sama* and *o-Tsuki-sama*.

"Those rascally legs, on the other hand..."

San and *Ichi* had put a box around the legs,

and *Ni* carried it back to where the others were.

"This is the number 4," explained Anji. "After all, there are two legs, so if you put them in a box that makes four, doesn't it?"

"Does it?" asked Arisu.

"Of course it does. We call her..."

"I know, I know," interrupted Arisu. "Her name is *Shi*."

"*Sh*," said Anji.

"*Sh*?" asked Arisu. "Not *Shi*?"

"I meant *Sh*. As in *Sshhh*. Be-quiet *sh*. We try not to say *Shi*. It means four but it also means death. So *Shi* is an Unlucky Number. Why do you think hotels often don't have a Room 4?"

"I didn't know they didn't."

"Kansas must be a strange place. We like to call poor *Shi* by another name. We call her *Yon* most of the time."

"Because her legs are always running off into the wild blue *Yon*der," said *San*.

"Always running hither and *Yon*," said *Ni*.

"No personal remarks, please," said Anji. "Let me introduce the next number. This is little *Go*. She is number 5."

"She looks rather like a 4-sandwich standing on her head," said Arisu and then hoped she hadn't made another personal remark.

"Well, if you put 4 in a sandwich and turn it upside down, obviously you get 5," said Anji.

"I... suppose so," said Arisu doubtfully.

"Well, 4 plus one sandwich, if that makes you happier."

"A sandwich always makes one happier, doesn't it?" said Arisu.

"To remember the pronunciation, all you need to do is remember that it takes Japanese people a little longer to start a race."

"Why is that?" asked Arisu.

"What do you say when you start a race?" asked Anji.

"One, two, three, GO!" said Arisu.

"Well, in Japanese we say:

One, two, three, four, GO—*Ichi ni san shi GO!*"

"Shouldn't that have been *yon*?" asked Arisu.

Anji blushed slightly. "Not for races," she said hastily. "Races are different. Now let's get on to number 6."

3

The Rad Hatter

Anji was looking around for number 6 when what looked like another pair of legs came running past.

"More legs on the loose!" exclaimed Arisu.

"Not at all," said Anji. "That is *Hachi*—number 8. You know katakana, don't you, Doroshii?"

"I'm not Doroshii, but I *do* know katakana," said Arisu rather proudly.

Anji looked mildly puzzled and then continued. "Well, katakana ハ *ha* came from dear *Hachi*. Hatched from *Hachi*, you might say. ハ *ha* ハ *ha*!"

"*Hachi*-kun isn't a Free Radical then. So why is he running around so wildly?" asked Arisu.

"Because I've lost my hat!" said *Hachi*. "It's blown off and now it's bowling all over the place!"

"It's right here," said *Yon*. "I'll block it for you." Sure enough, the hat rolled against big, square *Yon* and stopped.

It was a very distinguished-looking top hat and it looked like this:

THE RAD HATTER

"The hat, of course, is a Free Radical. That's why it blows around so much," explained Anji.

Hachi put his hat on and instantly transformed into another kanji.

"Ah. *This* is number 6," said Anji. "His name is *Roku*."

"So why does 8 with a hat on become 6?" asked Arisu.

"*Roku* is rather nervous, I am afraid. I suppose you have heard why 6 was afraid of 7?"

"Because 789 (seven ate nine)," replied Arisu, feeling rather pleased with herself.

"Exactly," replied Anji. "And of course it is the 8 part that really frightens *Roku* and makes him hide. If you cover 8 with a hat, *Roku* can come out to play."

"So *Roku* isn't steady as a rock?"

"I am when I have my hat," objected *Roku*.

"And did 7 really eat 9?" asked Arisu.

"*Nana*-chan? She wouldn't eat a fly," said Anji. "Would you, darling?"

"I certainly wouldn't," said *Nana*. "Flies are disgusting. *Roku*-kun sometimes looks a *little* bit yummy though."

"I'm not scared of you with my nice hat on," said *Roku*.

"And I wouldn't eat you with your cute hat on either," said *Nana*. And then seeing that *Roku* did look just a *teensy* bit scared, she added, "or even without it. You are my dear next-door friend, you know."

Roku smiled happily.

"Some Europeans put a cross through their 7s as you probably know," said Anji.

"They think it stops them from being mistaken for—I don't know—elephants or something. Unfortunately it doesn't stop them from turning upside down. Not that *Nana*-chan is upside down, of course. That is her natural appearance."

"I thought her name was *Shichi*," said Arisu.

"It is, but she is often called *Nana* too. I am not sure why. Perhaps because there is a bit of *Shi* in *Shichi*."

Arisu felt pleased because *Shichi* always felt a bit hard to say, and *Nana* seemed like a nicer name to her anyway.

九

"Hi there," said a kanji who looked a bit like a children's slide in the play park and had obviously become tired of waiting to be introduced. "You can call me *Ku* or *Kyuu*. I don't mind which."

"That's 'cause he's *ku-kuu*," murmured *Nana*-chan.

THE RAD HATTER

"Pleased to mee—*yoroshiku onegaishimasu*," said Arisu with a little bow.

"*Yoroshiku ne*. I'm number 9, and I'd like to see anyone try to eat *me*."

Arisu remembered that there were always at least 9 people in the *Kyuu* to get on the slide. Maybe that made *Kyuu*-kun a little self-important.

"This is my friend *Juu*. She's number 10. I'm practically a double figure myself so we get on well."

Juu smiled and bowed deeply. "*Yoroshiku onegaishimasu*. Welcome to Kanji Land, Arisu-sama," she said.

Arisu bowed as deeply and prettily as she knew how. And what was that thing you say? *Ko*cha? *Ko*chin?—ah yes, "*Kochira koso, yoroshiku onegaishimasu*," she said, feeling very proper indeed.

Juu smiled that very kind smile again.

"If I may say so, *Juu*-sama, you are a little like the Roman number 10 who looks like X."

"That's right. We are close cousins. But we like to keep things upright here in Kanji Land."

Even though *Juu* was a double figure, she didn't seem to be at all proud. As if in answer to Arisu's unspoken thought, *Juu* said, "Of course, I am *senpai* to all the single figures here. But you know we all have our own *senpai*. And there are some truly, truly distinguished kanji in the tower over there. Would you care to meet them?"

"Would that be all right? I mean, I'm only…"

"Of course it is all right," said *Juu*, smiling that lovely smile once more and extending one of her always-extended hands toward Arisu. "Let's go, shall we?"

4

The Tower of the Ancients

Juu led Arisu across the field to where she could see a great white stone tower rising into the clouds. Its pointed summit was of blazing gold, and flaming torches burned so brightly that they could be seen even against the bright blue summer sky. It stood on a small hill of deep, rich red earth in which grew the most lovely trees, and around it was a moat of the bluest, brightest water that Arisu had ever seen.

"What a beautiful tower," cried Arisu.

"Beautiful indeed, Arisu-sama," said *Juu*. "This is the Tower of the Ancients, and in it lie the foundations of all things."

"The foundations of...."

"You'll see when we get there. It is a very special place."

"Are you sure it's all right for me to..."

"Oh yes." That wonderful smile again.

When they reached the moat Arisu realized that there was no bridge.

"How do we cross?" she asked.

"You'll see," said *Juu* and then shouted aloud in her melodious voice, "*Shiro*-sama *yo!*"

Arisu heard a rippling of the water. From the other side of the moat a boat was being rowed toward them. It was rowed by a lady standing upright using a long oar. She was dressed all in white. Her long hair was pure white, although she looked young—or perhaps rather, ageless. Her face was as white as snow.

THE TOWER OF THE ANCIENTS

"This is *Shiro*, the Daughter of the Sun. As you see, she looks like *o-Hi-sama* except that there is a single drop above her. That is a drop of pure, pure light. All light comes from *Hi*, the sun, you know."

"Yes, I know," said Arisu.

"And if you have *pure* light in which all colors are perfectly contained, do you know what color that is?"

"Yes, yes!" cried Arisu. "It is white."

"Exactly. And this is *Shiro*, the Sheer White Maiden, the single perfect drop of light."

"Will *she row* us across the moat?"

"Of course. That is why she is called *Shiro*."

"Because *she rows*—and she rules all the whiteness of the world?"

"She does."

"So if I had a piece of white paper, would I call it *shiro*?"

"Well, it wouldn't be *Shiro* herself, would it? It would just be *like Shiro*. If a place was full of sunshine, you wouldn't call it a sun place, would you? You would call it *sunny*—sun-y—sun-like."

"Hmm, yes. But in Japanese?"

"Very similar. If something is white, it isn't Whiteness itself—not *Shiro* herself. It is *Shiro*-y, *shiroi*."

"The same with many other words. *Aka* is red, so a red thing is *aka-i*. You'll see a little later."

They reached the tower shore and a white door opened. *Shiro* extended her long white beautiful hand to usher them in.

They entered a chamber where an old lady was sitting on a white throne. She looked rather like *Shiro*, except that she was wearing a crown that looked like *Ichi*.

ALICE IN KANJI LAND

"*Hyaku*-sama," said *Juu*, bowing deeply.

"*Juu*-chan. How good to see you. How are the little ones?"

"They are all well, *senpai*. *Roku*-kun keeps losing his hat as usual."

Juu turned to Arisu. "This is *Hyaku*. The first great multiple of 10. That is why her hat is a 1. If you look at her sideways you can see her as a 1 and a pair of 0s. She is 100."

"That's very old," said Arisu.

"She isn't 100 years old. She is 100."

Hyaku laughed. "Don't look so surprised, *ojou-chan*. You've met people who are numbers before. What do you think *Juu*-chan here is? She's a very important number."

Juu blushed. "*Sonna koto... Senpai*, you know that you make ten of me."

"All numbers are important," said *Hyaku*. "Numbers were before there were things to be numbered. Numbers are the foundation of all things. That is why you met all the little numbers before you did anything else, *ojou-chan*.

"Very soon, you are going to meet the other foundations of all things. But I expect *Juu* will want to take you to see her brother *Sen* first."

As *Juu* and Arisu went up the stairs to the next chamber, *Juu* said, "The First Multiple of 10 is very pure. That is why she is so white and so closely related to *Shiro*. In fact, *Shiro* is often called *haku*—which is nearly *hyaku*—when she combines with others."

"She has two names?"

"Most kanji have two names. Some have more than two, though often only two are really important. One name is the regular name and the other is the glue-name."

"Glue-name?"

THE TOWER OF THE ANCIENTS

"Well, the proper word is *on-yomi* or on-reading, but the little ones call it their glue-name. It is the name they use when they stick to something. For example, *haku-chou* means white bird—a swan. *Haku-shi* is white paper. *Shiro*'s glue-name is *haku* because she and *Hyaku* are so closely related."

"My, that's a lot to remember!"

"As we're in Elementary right now, we'll mostly only learn the regular names. But when it's useful we'll learn some glue-names too. Here's *Sen-oniichan*'s room. *Sen* is 1000—but, uh, he doesn't always act his magnitude."

Juu knocked the door and a jaunty voice cried, "*Haitte!*" The two walked in.

Sen looked very like *Juu*, except that he was wearing a jaunty little hat tipped at a rakish angle.

Sen's room was decorated in bright colors, which felt surprising after the pure whiteness of *Shiro* and *Hyaku*.

"How do you do, *chibi-chan*? I'm *Sen*. Not as pure as *Hyaku* or as grand as *Man*. Just plain ol' *Sen*. But if you want a job done, sen' it to me. Hi-hiii. You see what I did there? *Sen* it to me!

"You like the hat? It's symbolic. I'm the highest multiple of 10 so I get capped off at the top. Don't worry though, I have a nice line in fancy hats and I always tilt them at just the right angle."

"The highest multiple of 10...?"

"Well, yes, *chibi-chan*—until you get to *Man*, of course. *Man*, that's somethin' else! Hi-hiii! See what I did there? *Man* is 10,000. *Man* has Special Significance. You'll meet *Man* later. I'm just *Sen*. I'm only 1,000. You drew the short straw meeting me!"

"On the contrary, it is a great honor to meet you, *Sen*-sama," said Arisu.

"The girl has manners! What's your name, girl?"

"Arisu *desu*."

"*Yoroshiku*, Arisu. I'm guessing you came to see the Five, did you?"

"The five what?" asked Arisu.

Sen burst out laughing. "And I thought I was funny. The five what? *The* Five, of course. The

Go-Gyou. The five travelers, the five movers, the five changers. (Don't worry, you'll get to that second kanji later). If it wasn't for those five there wouldn't be anything. Well, maybe numbers, because 'numbers were before there were things to be numbered'. I expect *Hyaku*-sama told you that."

"Yes, she did."

"Well, is that where you are going?"

Arisu looked at *Juu*, and *Juu* said, "Yes, it is. Would you do the honors, *Oniichan*?"

"But of course," said *Sen*. He waved his arms and all at once there seemed like more than two arms. There were ten, there were twenty, there were hundreds maybe. So many Arisu had no hope of counting them all, but she guessed it must be a thousand.

And the room seemed to melt away, giving place to a great marble dance floor. A strange dance was taking place. A great flame danced, throwing red light over all the room, then the flame was overcome by blue, blue water, and out of the water grew a glorious green tree. Shining gold came out of the rich brown earth, and the gold was melted by the great flame that had returned. It seemed like the dance of all nature, constantly coming to birth, growing, and dying. It seemed unbelievably beautiful and ecstatically happy and unbearably sad, all at the same time.

"Are there kanji even here?" asked Arisu.

"Look carefully and you'll see them," said *Juu*.

"Oh oh! That red one..."

"That's *Hi*, fire."
"The same name as the sun?"
"Fire is a little sun on earth, and the sun a great fire in the sky," said *Juu*.
"What about her shape?" asked Arisu.
"A human looks like this:

because a human is the upright being that walks on two legs. She is also the only being that can use fire, so fire shows a human with her arm extended, juggling a flame.

"Some say that humans have fire inside them, which is why they can use fire. Perhaps that is why a human is called *hito*. Fire is *hi* and humans are *hi too*!

"Can you see any other kanji?"
"The blue one!"

"That's *Mizu*, water. She is also called *Sui*. Some people call her Ms. Suey," —*Juu* pronounced Ms. as Mizu in the Japanese way— "but really her name is *Mizu*, and *Sui* is her glue-name.

"Her kanji shows a great waterspout rising out of the sea with splashes coming out on both sides."

"Oh, and that tree!"

"Isn't it magnificent? You can see the sturdy tall trunk and the wide spreading branches—and also the branches that come downward to give us lovely fruit. It is a very kind tree. All trees are kind, you know."

"What is its name?"

"Its name is *Ki*."

"What a simple name."

"Yes. *Ki* is one of the most basic things. *Ki* means tree, but as an element—one of the Great Five—*Ki* is all green and growing things. So you see, *Ki* is the *key* to all life."

"Oh, and the gold one!"

"Gold is exactly what it is. It is said *Kane* or *Kin*. When we say *o-kane* we mean money because money used to be all gold.

"The kanji for a monarch is

because traditionally a monarch is the person who stands at the Great Pillar between Earth and Heaven and brings Heavenly rule to Earth."

"What is the monarch called?"

"*Ou.*"

"Just *ou?*"

"Really just *ou.*"

"*Ou*—I mean oh."

"But we were talking about *Kin*, or *Kane*. If you look at her carefully

you can see the monarch in her house with two bars of gold."

"*Ou* yes, so you can! I mean oh. *Ou* dear, I've caught the habit."

"*Kin* or *kane* means gold but also means metal. That is because gold is the Mother of Metals. Therefore all other metals are part of her family. If you want to say metal clearly, you have to say *kin-zoku*—that means gold-family or metal-family. That way everyone knows you mean metal in general and not gold."

"So *Kin* is gold and other metals are her kin?"

"Exactly so. Can you see the last of the Great Five?"

"The brown one."

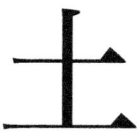

"Yes. That is *Tsuchi*, earth."

"She might look like a cross or a shovel stuck into the earth."

"Yes, or—well, I don't like to sound boastful, but…" *Juu* blushed a little, "well, 10 is often seen as the number of completion, representing, well, *everything*. And the ground is what everything rests on."

"Of course, of course!" shouted Arisu. "It's just like you, isn't it, only with the ground underneath you!"

Juu still seemed rather embarrassed. "We'd better go now," she said.

"Really?" said Arisu. "I feel as if I could watch the Dance of the Five for the rest of my life."

"Oh, you will," said *Juu*.

"What do you mean?"

"Here in Kanji Land or in the Human World or in any world at all, everything is the Dance of the Five. Without the Five there would be nothing."

"Except numbers?" asked Arisu.

Juu only smiled.

5

The Five Ways and Ten Thousand Things

Juu raised her right arm and traced a kanji in the air. For a moment it stood suspended there like a figure in golden light

and then they started going UP! Up and up and up into the air. *Go no Heya*—the Chamber of the Five—seemed to have no ceiling and the tower seemed to go up and up forever.

"That kanji," said Arisu, "was that *Tsuchi?*"

"It looked a tiny bit like her, didn't it? But if you look carefully you will see that she has no left arm. So you couldn't mistake her for me!"

"So who is it?"

"Can't you guess from what is happening to us? This is *Ue*. Her meaning is *up!*"

"Up and up and up! *Way* up!"

"*Way* up, exactly. *Ue* is the way *up*. She rises from the ground a bit like a flag. Her sister drops down *under* the ground like a droopy flag. We'll meet her in a short while. But right now we're going way, way, way up."

The glowing kanji spoke. "I don't *only* mean up, you know. I also mean up-on."

"Up-on?" asked Arisu.

"Yes, up-on. Upon. As in 'The book is upon the table'. So I belong to everything."

"You *belong* to *everything?*" repeated Arisu in a puzzled voice.

"Exactly. If you want to say, 'The book is on the table' (a very silly way of putting it if you ask me), you say *hon wa teeburu no **ue** ni aru*—'The book is at the table's upon.' Every thing has an upon, a *ue*."

"Everything?"

"Everything. Your head, for example. Your head's *ue* is where you put your hat. The grass's *ue* is where you sit and have a picnic. Your nose's *ue* is where your glasses would sit—if you had glasses."

"That's *ue* cool!" said Arisu.

Ue and *ue*—I mean, up and up—they went, until they came to the very top of the tower, where they could see for miles over the whole of Kanji Land.

And there at the very top was a kanji that shone in all the colors of the rainbow. It looked like this:

"Why, isn't that little *Ichi* at the top? The very first kanji I met?"

"That's right, it is."

"And underneath her? It looks like a letter h…."

"Or you can see it as a wrapper. The *Tao Te Ching* tells us that the Ten Thousand Things are wrapped into One."

"The Ten Thousand Things?"

"Yes, this is *Man*—ten thousand. But ten thousand also means—well, just everything—huge, innumerable amounts of things. It is the same in Greek. *Myriad* meant literally ten thousand, but figuratively—uncountable muchness."

"So that's why *Sen* said, '*Man*, that's somethin' else'."

"That's right. *Man* is more than a number—in a way. Though she is more often literally 10,000 these days."

"Look you out over the country," said *Man* unexpectedly. "There shall you see the Ten Thousand Things. The small and the great, the breathing and the still. The wind and the water and the verdant valley."

For a moment Arisu looked out over the Ten Thousand Things of Kanji Land.

"You can't see them properly from here, but you soon will," said *Juu*. "One by one you can see each, but you can't see all. From here, with *Man*, you can see all, but not each."

"*Man* really *is* something else, isn't she?"

"*Man* is *everything* else. If you want, you can see the kanji as *h* for hundred plus *one*. If we say 'a hundred' we mean literally a hundred, but if we say 'a hundred and one' we mean 'lots and lots'. Like the ten thousand!"

"*Man*, *Sen*, *Hyaku*: I hope I remember who is who."

"Well, *Hyaku* starts with *H* for *Hundred*, *Sen* starts with *S* for *Sousand*…"

"Sousand?"

"There is no 'th' sound in Japanese, so in foreign words it gets pronounced 's' as in *sankyuu*—thank you."

"Ah, I see. What about *Man*?"

"Well, *Man* starts with *M* for *Million*."

"But *Man* isn't a million…"

"No, but she is the big number after a thousand. Japanese has no special word for million, just as English has no special word for ten thousand. So the next big one after thousand starts with M in both."

"Well, that makes sense—in a Kanji Land kind of way," thought Arisu.

"Time to go down," said *Juu*, and she traced another golden kanji in the air:

and they started going down and down from the tower. Down and down and down.

"Is this *Ue*'s sister, down?" asked Arisu.

"That's right. Her name is *Shita*—or *Sita* depending how you write it in Romaji."

"*Way* up and *Sit-a*-down. But her flag is drooping."

"That's gravity, of course. Nothing to keep it *up*."

"And does everything have a *shita* just as everything has a *ue*?"

"Of course it does!" said *Shita*. "A thing's *ue* is its upon. A thing's *shita* is its underneath. A table's *shita* is where you hide. And all the ten thousand things you will see in Kanji Land are in *sora no shita*—the sky's underneath."

Down and down they went until they landed on the grass.

"Where do we go now?" asked Arisu.

"Let's look at the signpost," suggested *Juu*.

Sure enough, there was a wooden signpost with pointers pointing in two opposite directions, and sitting on the two pointers, facing in opposite directions, were two kanji:

"Who are these?" asked Arisu.

"That's *Migi* the Midget," said the one on the left, pointing at the one on the right.

"That's *Hidari* the Hideous," said the one on the right, pointing at the one on the left.

"You look rather alike," said Arisu.

"Alike?" said the one on the left. "I'm no *midget*."

"Alike?" said the one on the right. "I'm not *hideous*."

"But how do I tell you apart?" asked Arisu.

"These two are *complex kanji*," explained *Juu*. "They are made up of more than one element. So to understand them, let's look first at their parts.

"You see the long crossing lines at the left and top? They make a hand. Naturally, left and right both have a hand because we talk about right-*hand* side and left-*hand* side, don't we?

THE FIVE WAYS AND TEN THOUSAND THINGS

"There are several hand-elements in kanji. This one we call the Hand of Friendship. It is the one we find in

Tomo-dachi, friend. *Tomo* has two hands: the Hand of Friendship on the left and a regular hand radical

underneath it. *Tomo* is always holding hands. *Tomo* is super friendly."

"I always hoped I would find a true friend *tomo*rrow," said Arisu, a little sadly.

"Well, you've found *Tomo* today!" said *Juu*.

"But these two don't look very friendly," whispered Arisu. And then blushed because they had clearly heard her.

"Of course we're friendly," said *Migi*.

"Friendly as peas in a pod," said *Hidari*.

"It's our Act, you see," explained *Migi*.

"Left and Right always have to seem opposed to each other," said *Hidari*.

"But when we're offstage, we're as friendly as cheese and chocolate," said *Migi*.

"Of course, we aren't often offstage," added *Hidari*.

"But that's show biz," said *Migi*.

"But how do I tell them apart?" asked Arisu again.

"Let's look at what the hands are holding.

"*Hidari* is holding

which means craft, skill or carpentry. We don't often see her on her own, but we see her in words like

Dai-ku, which means carpenter. In the old days carpentry was the most important skill. The first of those two kanji means big, and you'll be meeting him in a few minutes."

"I suppose it takes a lot of carpenters to build a dyke."

"I don't know if it does, but if it helps you remember, that's splendid. You can also see the kanji as the end-on view of a girder used in building."

"So *Hidari* is left, and her hand is holding craft or skill. But surely the *right* hand is the skillful one…"

"Well, let's see what *Migi* is holding.

THE FIVE WAYS AND TEN THOUSAND THINGS

"This is *Kuchi*-chan. She is rather famous."

The square kanji made a modest bow. "I am but a humble player," she said.

"What do you play?" asked Arisu, thinking of trombones or chess.

"I play anything," said *Kuchi*. "Queens and commoners, saints and scoundrels. Tragedy and comedy, sublimity and farce." She giggled.

"Oh, an actress," said Arisu.

"I think 'player' sounds more dignified. Anyway. I am a mouth. My name is *Kuchi*."

"Because the easiest way to make someone open her mouth is to tickle her—*koochi*-KOOOO."

Kuchi rolled her eyes. "I suppose I did say farce," she sighed.

"To proceed," said *Juu* hastily, "we have *Hidari*, left, with hand and craft. *Migi*, right, with hand and mouth."

"But I still think right is usually the skillful, crafty hand," objected Arisu.

"Hmf. *Migi* is the Dominant Hand, so I *make* things and he *eats* them. That's the truth of the matter," said *Hidari*.

"The real truth is that *Hidari* can *do* some things but I am the skillful one so I always have to *tell* him what to do."

"Oh dear. Left and Right can never agree unless they meet in the…"

"Middle?" said Arisu.

"Yes, middle. This is a mouth with a line right through the middle."
"You notice they need *my* mouth to make middle," said *Migi*.
"I already have a middle-line on my craft," said *Hidari*.
"The middle kanji is called *Naka*," said *Juu*.
"Because she has the *knack'a* bringing left and right together?"
"She has the *knack'a* joining them all," said *Juu*.
"All?" asked Arisu.
"All four.

"*Ue, Shita, Migi, Hidari*. Up, Down, Left and Right. And *Naka* in the middle."

"And does everything have a left and a right the way everything has an upon and an underneath?"

"Yes, and a middle too and an inside, which is the same word as middle in Japanese. English has those last ones too. In English they say:

On the left of the table
On the right of the table
In the middle of the table
On the table
Under the table
In the box

So it's quite hard to learn. Different for almost all of them.

"Luckily, Japanese works the same all the time:

Teeburu no hidari ni—on the left of the table
Teeburu no migi ni—on the right of the table
Teeburu no naka ni—in the middle of the table
Teeburu no ue ni—on the table
Teeburu no shita ni—under the table
Hako no naka ni—in the box

Once we've learned the words, we don't need to learn a different way of using each one."

"Japanese is very logical, isn't it?"

"Very logical. If you approach it the right way, it makes much more sense than most human languages."

"What is the right way?" asked Arisu.

"From the right, of course," said *Migi*.

"From the left, naturally," said *Hidari*.

6

The Middle Way

"Which way should we go now?" asked Arisu.

"I think we should take the Middle Way," said *Juu*.

Arisu looked at the signpost again and saw that as well as *Migi* and *Hidari* pointing right and left, there was little *Naka* pointing to a road that ran straight between them.

The Middle Way was a curious road because the landscape on either side of it was so different. To the left were hills covered in green grass with bright red flowers. To the right the ground was level red earth with green trees and ferns growing from it. The left side looked shady and cool, and the right side looked sunny and warm.

As they walked on they saw a very big kanji on the right side of the road. By far the biggest kanji Arisu had seen so far:

"Why, that looks like *Hito*, person," said Arisu.

"Except he has his arms out wide."

"It was *this* big!" said the kanji, extending his arms even further.

"What was this big?" asked Arisu.

"Everything," said the kanji. "Big, Big, Big. My name's *Dai* by the way. Because if I got any bigger I'd *die*!"

"*Dai*-san, *yoroshiku onegaishimasu*," said Arisu.

"*Yoroshiku, yoroshiku*," said *Dai*. "To be honest, *Dai* is my glue-name, but everyone calls me *Dai*."

"May I ask what is your regular name?"

"*Ookii*," said *Dai*.

"Ooky," asked Arisu. "Like the Addams Family?"

"Not uuki, *ookii*. Rhymes with 'smokey', kinda. But keep that 'oo' long. And the 'ii' too."

"What does *ookii* mean?" asked Arisu.

"What do you think it means? It means big. I mean BIG." *Dai* spread his arms even wider. "It was THIS BIG."

Over on the cool side of the road was a teensy-tiny kanji. At first Arisu could hardly see her. She looked like this:

"*Sumimasen*, I didn't see you there," said Arisu.

"Nobody does. I'm small."

"You are small. You look like a tiny baby penguin to me. What is your name?" asked Arisu very gently. She felt that if she spoke too loud it might blow the tiny penguin-kanji away.

"I'm called *Shou*," she said.

"*Yoroshiku, Shou*-chan," said Arisu. She thought *Shou* was a rather ironic name because she didn't *show* much at all, she was so tiny. You could easily miss her. But she didn't say that, as it might be a Personal Remark.

"Of course, *Shou* is my glue-name, but everyone calls me that."

"What is your regular name?" asked Arisu.

"Why, it's

Chiisai," she said.

"*Chiisai*," said Arisu. "Like when someone gives you a tiny piece of *cheese* and it's barely enough to put in your *eye*."

"What a silly remark," said *Shou*. "Anyway, it isn't *cheese* with a Z. It rhymes with *geese* with an S. *Chii-sai*."

"Cheese doesn't have a Z," pointed out Arisu.

"It is *pronounced* Z," said *Shou*. "*Eigo wa baka ne*."

"*Chiisai*," said Arisu as correctly as she could, because *Shou* seemed to be getting a *chiisai* bit grumpy.

"That's better," said *Shou*. "Cheese in your eye! I never heard such silliness. But you are rather fun!"

"We must be moving along now," said *Juu*.

"But *Dai* and *Shou*—we've only just met them."

"Don't worry about that," said *Juu*. "You'll be seeing them again pretty soon."

They walked on along the strange road between two landscapes, and soon, on the right, they saw

"Why, that one looks like *hito* too!" said Arisu.

THE MIDDLE WAY

"A little, but look how the right stroke comes over the top of the left one."

"What does it mean?"

"It means going in."

"Going in what?"

"Going in anything. Going in a house, going in a forest. Three beans going in a bag. A mouse going in its hole. Going in anything."

"Oh yes, I see. So it is a person with a little whoosh-line at the top showing that she is zooming *into* something. "

"That's right," said *Juu*.

"How is it said?" asked Arisu.

"*Iru* or *hairu*. That is the verb, go in. *Iri* is the noun, entry. Here's *iru* or *hairu*. You can say this one either way."

"So *i-ru* is like *in-ru*, and when you go in you say '*hi*'!"

"That's right. Now let's see what happens when we combine *iru* with our old friend *Kuchi*, mouth:

What do you think that means?"

"Going-in mouth?" asked Arisu.

"Exactly right!" said *Juu*.

"But… I still don't know what it *means*," said Arisu.

"It means entrance," said *Juu*. "A mouth or opening that you go into."

"Entry-mouth," said Arisu.

"Yes," said *Juu*.

"So is it said *irikuchi*?" asked Arisu.

"Almost," said *Juu*. "It is actually said *iriguchi*."

"Why does *kuchi* turn into *guchi*?"

"It is called *rendaku*," said *Juu*, "and it's easier to understand when you look at the hiragana:

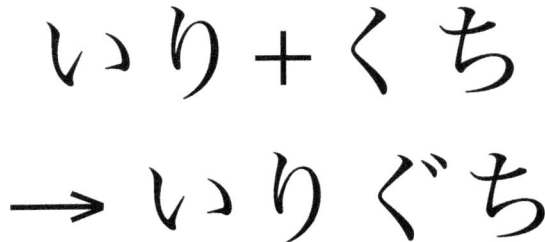

"When two words join together and the second one starts with a sharp sound like T or K or S, that sharp or clear sound becomes a soft or cloudy sound. In hiragana that just means that we put a little ten-ten on it:

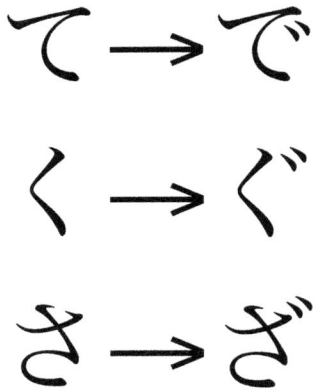

and so on. You will also see

etcetera in the *ha, hi, hu, he, ho* column."

"So the soft, cloudy ten-ten version is the glue-together form?"

"That's right. *Ren* means connect or join, and *daku* means cloudy or voiced sound (the softer ten-ten-ed sound). That's why it's called *rendaku*—join-cloudy."

"That's a hard word," muttered Arisu.

"It is, and you don't need to learn it."

"And the ten-ten, *ne*—in those *renny-ronny*..."

"*Rendaku.*"

"Yes, those. In those words the ten-ten is like two little hooks that hook the two together."

"Exactly so."

"So instead of *ren*... *dicky-dacky*—that thing—we could call it ten-ten hooking."

"Yes, let's call it that," agreed *Juu*. "Now let's see who is on the other side of the road."

On the shady side stood another kanji who looked like this:

"This one is..."

"Let me guess," said Arisu. "It is on the opposite side of the Middle Way from going-in, so it must be coming-out."

"Exactly right. To explain her, let's meet another friend." *Juu* drew a kanji in the air.

"This kanji means mountain. Because what things does a mountain have?"

"A mountain? Well, I suppose it has a peak, and a base, and sides…"

"That's right. So this kanji is the simplest kind of mountain. The long vertical line is the peak, the horizontal line is the base, and the two shorter vertical lines are the sides. Her name is *Yama*."

"Oh yes! Like Fuji-yama, Mount Fuji."

"Oh dear. You shouldn't say Fuji-yama."

"Why not?"

"It's a mistake. Foreigners say Fuji-yama because they see the mountain kanji in the name and know it is pronounced *yama*. But we don't say Fuji-*yama*, we say Fuji-*san*."

"Oh, I see. To be polite to the Sacred Mountain?"

"Well, of course one should be polite, but that isn't the reason. This *san* isn't the *san* that you add to a person's name. It is the glue-name of *yama*. So when we stick *yama* onto something else, like Fuji, it turns into *san*.

"Now, do you know how mountains were formed?"

"Hmm… I think it's something about the earth's core and the earth's crust and…"

"No, no. That's not it at all. In the beginning there was only one mountain, and that was Fuji-san, of course. One day Fuji-san got lonely and boinged another mountain right out of her summit. Later on that mountain boinged another mountain out of *her* summit, and so on. That is why there are lots of mountains today.

"And that is why

THE MIDDLE WAY

means coming out. It is a picture of one mountain boinging another mountain out of her summit.

"The usual sound of coming out is *de*. Like de-parting, de-camping or de-fenestrating."

"*Defenestrating?*"

"It means throwing someone out of a window."

"I don't believe it."

"Look it up."

"So *de* is going out or coming out."

"That's right. So how do you think you would say 'go out'?"

"Umm…

deru?"

"Precisely. And what do you think this is?"

"It means exit," said Arisu.

"*Pin-pon! Pin-pon!* Exactly right."

"And it is said *deriguchi*."

"Not quite. It is said *deguchi*."

"Why isn't it *deriguchi* when *iriguchi* is *iriguchi*?" asked Arisu a little grumpily. "Is it one of those silly things you just have to guess?"

"No, it isn't," said *Juu*. "But you'll need a little more grammar to understand why. So for now let's just remember *deguchi* and *iriguchi*." She smiled that wonderful smile and Arisu's grumpiness melted away like springtime snow.

"Before we move on I'd like to introduce two friends who will help us in a moment," said *Juu*. She drew a kanji in the air:

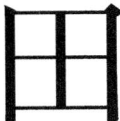

"This is a field," she said. "Imagine a field plowed longwise and crosswise. Or a chessboard (which is a field of action)."

"What is it called?"

"*Ta*, or *da* in its ten-ten hook form."

"Because Dada used to work in the fields?"

"Very true. In fact you will be seeing more about that very thing shortly. But first let's meet our second new friend."

"Why, it looks practically the same as a katakana KA."

"That's right. And it means *strength*. Obviously KA is the strongest character in KAtaKAna because it appears twice in the name."

"And is it pronounced KA too?"

"Well, no, but it has KA in the middle. It is pronounced *chiKAra*."

"Why?"

"Obviously a *chick-carrier* can carry a lot of chicks so he must be very strong."

"I would have said an ox-carrier or an elephant-carrier would be stronger than a chick-carrier."

"Really! Whoever heard of an ox-carrier or an elephant-carrier? In the old days chicks were packed in big wooden crates and the chick-carriers carried dozens at a time. So their strength was enormous.

"Of course, nowadays chicks are carried in KArs so it is much easier all around. But the KArs still have to be *strong*.

"And now we are ready to move on."

They walked a little further down the Middle Way, and on the right side of the road they saw a new kanji that looked like this:

"Why, that's the two we just learned joined together, *ta/da*—field and *chikara*—strength."

"That's right. And it means male, because…"

"I know, I know! Because in the old days *strong men* used to work in the *fields*."

"That's right. It is pronounced *otoko*. After Otto & Co., the all-male company of *strong field-workers*.

"*Sore de wa*, Test Time!" announced *Juu* briskly. "What do you make of this? No unexpected pronunciations, so I think you can get it right first time."

"Why that's... it must be... *Otoko no hito*, and it means male person—man."

"*Pin-pon, pin-pon, pin-pon!* One hundred percent!" cried *Juu*. "We can regard this as a single word. *Otokonohito*, man. The *no* is the possessive particle, so literally it means male's person."

"Male's person?"

"Person *belonging to* (the class) male. Lots and lots of words and expressions work like that. For example, if we wanted to say 'Fifi the cat' we would say *Neko no Fifi* = 'cat's Fifi' = Fifi belonging to (the class) cat."

But Arisu had become distracted.

"Oh, look, on the other side of the road…

It must be…"

"That's right," said *Juu*. "Since she's on the opposite side to *Otoko*, she must be female. The kanji is said to depict a woman sitting with crossed legs or a woman dancing.

"It is pronounced *onna*, because everyone knows that Japanese women are people of the highest *honor*.

"But of course it doesn't mean woman by itself; it just means female. How would you make it mean woman?"

"I know! I know!" said Arisu.

"*Onna no hito*."

"Direct hit! Going down the Middle Way has really given you the *naka* of combined-kanji words, hasn't it?"

7

The Child with Six Fingers

Arisu and *Juu* reached the end of the Middle Way and found themselves in a place where there were hills *and* level ground, sunshine *and* shade, trees *and* flowers.

And the first person they met was a little child. Her head was large in relation to her body, like an anime child, and her arms were stretched out welcomingly, just like *Juu*'s.

"Why, it's little *Ko*," said *Juu*.

"*Yahho!*" cried *Ko*.

"This is Arisu," said *Juu*. "Do your *jikoshoukai* (self-introduction), *Ko*-chan."

"*Ko de~su*. My full name is *Sushiko* 'cause that's all my names, *Su*, *Shi* and *Ko*. But people just say *Ko* most of the time. *Yoroshiku*, Arisu-chan."

"*Yoroshiku, Ko*-chan."

"Why don't you show Arisu-chan some of the words you can make?"

"*Un*. How about this?"

"What's that, Arisu?"
"That must be... Yes! *Onna no ko*—girl."
"How about this one?" said *Kō*.

"*Otoko no ko*—boy."
"It's easy when you know how, isn't it?" said *Juu*. "Now let's play Body Parts. I'll point to a part of me, and you two make the kanji."

Juu pointed to her mouth, and Arisu quickly made the kanji in the air:

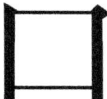

"Good. You might need *Kō*-chan to help you with the rest, though." She pointed to her eye, and *Kō*-chan made a kanji in the air. It looked like this:

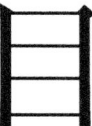

"It almost looks like *o-Hi-sama*," said Arisu.
"All light comes from *o-Hi-sama*, and the only way we can see light is with our eye. So if *o-Hi-sama* is light number one, the eye is light number two."
"Oh yes, they have *Ichi* and *Ni* in their middles, don't they!"

"That's right. Or if you prefer, you could think of the kanji on its side and remember that round things become square. Then you can see it as an oval shape with a circle in the middle—an eye."

"What is an eye called?"

"*Me*," cried *Ko*-chan.

"You?" said Arisu.

"Not U, *me*," said *Ko*-chan.

Arisu was confused. "What is eye?" she asked.

"You mean what *am* I," said *Ko*-chan.

"Not *me, eye*."

"But eye *is* me," said *Ko*-chan, looking rather frustrated.

"The word for eye is *me*," explained *Juu*. "But you don't pronounce it like the English word 'me'."

"How do you pronounce it?" asked Arisu.

"Meh," said *Ko*-chan.

"There's no need to be grumpy," said Arisu.

"I'm not being grumpy. That's how you pronounce it. Meh."

"Let's get on with the game," said *Juu* hastily, and she pointed to her hand. Ko drew

"It looks just like a hand," said Arisu, "only…"

"Only what?" asked *Juu*.

"Only it's got six fingers," said Arisu.

"Of course," said *Ko*-chan. "Hands do, you know. Haven't you ever noticed?"

Ko held out her hand, and sure enough, it had six fingers.

Arisu looked at her hand and then held it out.

"Oh, you poor thing!" said *Ko*-chan. "Whatever happened?"

"She's *human*," said *Juu*. "They only have five."

"The poor *things*!" said *Ko*-chan.

"We've already met two hands," said Arisu, changing the subject quickly. "In friendship."

"But this one is the hand that stands alone, when we just want to say 'hand'," said *Juu*.

"The hand that stands alone. How can a hand stand?"

"You've never heard of a handstand?" asked *Ko*.

"I guess I have," said Arisu, "now I come to think of it."

"Hand is called *Te*," said *Juu*.

"*Me* and *Te*, eye and hand," said Arisu. "I is me and hand makes tea. Only you say them *meh* and *teh*.

"Or—if you take TE and turn the E on its side and put it on top of the T you have a picture of a hand!"

"Just so. And now…" *Juu* pointed to her ear.

Quick as a blink, *Ko*-chan drew the kanji:

"Why, that's like *Me*—only…"

"Only with hair all around it," said *Ko*. "We get to know everything through our eyes and ears. Our eyes stand out in front, but our ears are around the side with hair all around them."

"Does ear have an *-e* name like *Me* and *Te*?" asked Arisu.

"Oh no, ear is *Mimi*," said *Juu*.

"Like Screaming Mimi," said *Ko*. "Only Screaming Mimi makes us *cover* our ears."

THE CHILD WITH SIX FINGERS

"I don't think I want to meet Screaming Mimi," said Arisu.

Juu pointed to her foot, and *Ko* made another kanji in the air:

"I can't say that looks a great deal like a foot," said Arisu.

"Let's meet someone else before we talk about her," said *Juu*, and made a kanji of her own in the air:

"This one means stop. At one time apparently it meant foot, because it looked like a foot."

"It doesn't look like a foot to me," said *Ko*, "but I suppose humans have funny feet just like their funny hands."

"No personal remarks, please," said *Juu*. "Anyway, let's just see it as a child (the short vertical) on the road (the bottom horizontal) beside a policeman who is holding out his hand (the long vertical and short horizontal) to stop the traffic so the child can cross."

"How is it said?" asked Arisu.

"On its own it isn't said. But the main word is *tomeru*," said *Juu*.

ALICE IN KANJI LAND

"*Tom* is the name of the policeman that stops traffic, you see," said *Ko*.

"So back to foot, as the man said when his car was stolen," said *Juu*.

"He should have called *Tom*," said *Ko*.

Juu drew the kanji again:

"You see *Kuchi* is at the top and *Tom* at the bottom. I know *Tom* looks a bit different here, but this is his underneath-form. Now why anyone ever thought *Tom* looks like a foot I don't know…"

"Except that policemen have big feet," put in *Ko*.

"…but we can say that when you put your foot in your mouth you need to stop talking. So foot is a *mouth-stop*."

"What is foot called?" asked Arisu.

"*Ashi*," said *Juu*. "And *Ashi* can mean either foot *or* leg. You might know that Cinderella got her name from the fact that she had to kneel in the cinders of the fireplace, cleaning it or making the fire. In fact, in the Grimms' German version she is called Aschenputtel (*Aschen* means ashes in German). As you can imagine, she got her legs and feet all ashy."

"Some people say she slept there and got ashy all over," said *Ko*.

"That's right," said *Juu*. "And she was only saved because of the slipper that fell from her *foot*."

8

Kin-Kon-KAN-Kon

Kin-kon-KAN-kon. A school chime could be heard in the distance.

"Oh dear, I have to zoom, or I'll be late," said *Ko*. "Why don't you come too, Arisu-chan?"

Arisu looked at *Juu*. "Is that all right?" she asked.

"Of course," said *Juu*. "I'll see you again later."

The two girls ran along the road until they reached a little schoolhouse with a little clock tower on the roof. Lots of little kanji were going in and Arisu followed *Ko* into the building.

The teacher was a large rabbit in a blue dress with a yellow ribbon at the base of one ear. Her ears were very large even for a rabbit. She looked at Arisu a little quizzically.

"She's human," whispered *Ko*.

"*Naruhodo*," said the teacher. And then turning to Arisu, "My name is Mimi-sensei, because, well, I am rather proud of my ears. Please go to the chalkboard and do your *jikoshoukai*, little human girl."

Arisu walked up to the chalkboard. All the little kanji fell silent watching her and she started to feel very self-conscious. However, she had seen scenes like this in anime, so she knew just what to do.

She picked up a stick of chalk and wrote

on the board.

"*Watashi wa Arisu desu*. I came from Human World by falling into a book. As it happens, I was trying to walk to Japan, but I am glad I came here and I want to learn all about you kanji-peoples."

She made a deep bow and said "*Yoroshiku onegaishimasu.*" The whole class broke into applause.

"You can sit over there, next to *Kō*-chan," said Mimi-sensei, and Arisu went to her seat. Everyone was chattering *gaya-gaya* about the new student. But Mimi-sensei rapped on her desk.

"*Mina-san, shizuka ni!*" she shouted, and everyone fell silent. "Today we are going to learn about colors. Who knows how to write the color white?"

Several hands went up, including Arisu's. Mimi-sensei invited Arisu to the chalkboard, and she wrote *Shiro*:

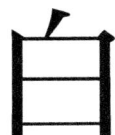

"Very good," said Mimi-sensei. "Now can you write the color red?" Arisu couldn't write red, but she went it. "I'm afraid not," she said. "Who can?" asked Mimi-sensei.

Kō-chan put her hand up. She went to the board and wrote:

"Correct," said Mimi-sensei. "In English we call this 'Red, AKA Scarlet'. In Japanese we just call it 'AKA' which is shorter. If we want to say that *something* is red, we say *aka-i*."

"Just the same as white," said Arisu.

"That's right," said Mimi-sensei.

"Now let's look at how *Aka* is made up. The part at the top is easy, isn't it? That is

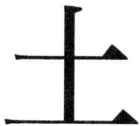

our old friend *Tsuchi*, earth. But what is underneath?" She wrote another kanji:

"This is *Katana*. Who knows what *Katana* means?"

"I know," said Arisu. "It's a Japanese sword."

"That's right," said Mimi-sensei. "This kanji seems to show just the grip and the handguard. Possibly because it is a ninja *katana*, so the blade is invisible.

"I am sure you have noticed how red the earth is around here. Just imagine if you thrust a *katana* into the earth and red blood flowed out. You can see two streams of it coming out in the *Aka* kanji, can't you? Don't worry, though. You can't hurt the earth. Not with a *katana*, anyway.

"So, suppose you wanted to say 'red tree'. How do you think you would say it, Arisu?"

"*Akai ki*," said Arisu.

"That's right," said Mimi-sensei. "We have *Aka*, red, *i* to show that *something* is red, and *Ki*, tree. A red-y tree.

"How about blue?"

This time no hands went up, and Mimi-sensei wrote on the board:

"Now once again, I think we have one element we know well and another that we don't yet know. The known element is, of course, dear *Tsuki*, the moon. The other one is not a kanji on its own, but it is closely related to

"This one means life, or birth, or growing up. It is usually pronounced *Sei*, which sounds like 'say'. Because every time you see your aunt from over the mountain, she says…"

Several hands shot up at once. "Go ahead," said Mimi-sensei.

"*Say*, you have grown since I saw you last," chimed the class in unison. And all started laughing.

"*Shizuka ni!*" shouted Mimi-sensei. "Let's think about *why* the *Sei* kanji means life or birth or growing up. It looks like one of those charts you stand against to have your height measured, doesn't it? Growing up you go from little to bigger to bigly-big. And that little drop there—why, that is you. The tiny bit of you-ness that is the same in the little baby that can't speak a word, in the growing-up child you are now, in the adult, and in the old, old person.

"So, why does blue look like this?"

"The answer is obvious, isn't it? People who are *born and live* on the *moon* are blue. Martians are green, but Moon-people are blue."

Arisu's hand shot up.

"Yes, Arisu?"

"So why can people with big-huge telescopes not see the blue people on the moon?"

"That is because they mostly live under the moon's surface in burrows. Like rabbits. Every now and again they all come to the surface at once and the moon looks blue. But that doesn't happen very often."

"Only once in a blue moon?" asked Arisu.

"Exactly. And blue is pronounced *ao*."

"Is that because when you fall over and hurt your knee it turns blue and you say *ao*?" asked *Ko*-chan.

"Possibly, but I believe the more likely explanation is that just as we are surrounded by blue—the blue sky and the blue seas—so the vowels are also surrounded by blue:

AIUEO—you see, AO is at the beginning and the end. The alpha and the omega, you might say. We are surrounded by blue.

"Now, if we wanted to say 'blue moon', how do you think we would say it?"

Ko-chan shot up her hand and wrote:

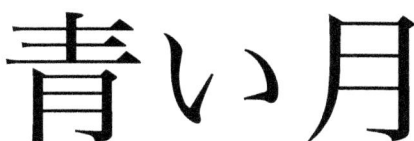

"*Aoi tsuki*," she said.

"That's right. You pop that *i* in there to show that *something* is *ao*. What you are doing is turning the noun *ao* into the i-adjective *aoi*. But that is for grammar class. Now, who can tell me what this is?"

ALICE IN KANJI LAND

"It's me! It's me!" squeaked *Ko*-chan excitedly.

"Well, part of it is you," said Mimi-sensei. "But you'll notice that she is wearing a shining crown."

"Yes! I want one!" said *Ko*-chan.

"It is the crown of study and learning. So if you wear that you have to do an awful lot of homework."

"Oh—well, maybe I don't want it after all," said *Ko*-chan.

"More precisely, it is what is called a wa-shaped crown, topped off by a very little little."

"A very little little?" asked the children. "A wa-shaped crown?"

"The top-element

is a compressed version of *Shou:*

But I often prefer to think of her as 'shining'."

"Oh, the little penguin puts her wings up in her even-tinier version of *Shou*," said Arisu.

"*Kawaii!*" said the whole class.

Mimi-sensei continued, "And this

is a wa-shaped crown. So called because it looks a bit like a katakana WA. But we can just think of it as the Crown. Both of them are Free Radicals but quite tame ones. They don't usually run all over the place like some I could mention.

"Now, when you put together the wa-shaped crown and the little little you get the Shining Crown of Learning. You will see this in other kanji too.

"A child wearing the Shining Crown means study or learning or school, and it is pronounced *gaku*.

"You don't often see *Gaku* on her own, but she pairs up with other kanji to make lots of words. Some of them we can make already. Let's try.

"How do you think you might say this?"

"*Shou-gaku?*" asked Arisu.

"That's right. *Shougaku*. Little-school. It means Elementary School. Where we are right now.

"Let's try another."

"Why, that must be Middle School," said *Ko*-chan.

"That's right," said Mimi-sensei.

"And is it said *Naka-gaku*?" asked Arisu.

"Not quite," said Mimi-sensei. "*Shou* is the glue-name of *Chii(sai)*. Since we are joining kanji, we need the glue-name of *Naka*. And that is *Chuu*. Because we chew things *inside* our mouth. At least we should."

"*Chuu-gaku*, then?" said *Ko*.

"That's right. *Chuugaku*—Middle School.

"How about this?"

"*Dai-gaku!*" said Arisu.

"That's right. *Daigaku*. Big-school—it doesn't mean High School, mind, but University. What about this?"

"*Gaku-sei?*" suggested *Ko*.

"Yes, *gakusei*. Someone living the life of learning. A student.

"Now let's try one everyone learned a while back."

"That must mean going into school," said Arisu.

"That's right. Specifically, it means entering a school for the first time or entering a new school. And it is pronounced *nyuu-gaku*."

"Oh, new school, *nyuu gaku*. Just like English."

"Actually, *nyuu* is the glue-name of *iru/hairu*. But if we remember *nyuugaku*—joining a *new school*—we won't forget it, will we?"

"We can really make a lot of words with the kanji we know already, can't we, Sensei?"

"Yes, we can. And we will be able to make more and more as we progress."

"Yay!" shouted Arisu.

"Here is the kanji for father:

Probably because Father was fond of having crossed swords displayed on the wall, while Mother preferred flowery wallpaper.

"Father was very fashionable and always wore his top hat when he went out. He didn't wear shoes though, because his toes were very big, which is why he was called o-toe-san. Or to spell it properly, *o-tou-san*.

"So that's Father with his crossed swords, and here is Mother with her wallpaper divided into little squares with a flower in each square."

"I'm not sure it looks like wallpaper," whispered *Ko*-chan.

"Some people see it as the two breasts of a breast-feeding mother," said Mimi-sensei. "Others see it as a double baby-carriage with a baby in each compartment, pushed by Mother of course.

"Mother is called

o-kaa-san. For very obvious reasons."

"What reasons?" asked Arisu.

"Well, who do you think ferries the children around in the car? In English they call it Mom's Taxi. In Japanese they call her o-car-san.

"But back to the story. Mother used to teach the children at home. The first school outside the home was started by Father who put on his top hat:

Yes, *that* Free Radical top hat. I don't know how long he had to chase it before he caught it.

"Once he had his top hat on he went out among the trees and started teaching. And that was the first school.

It is pronounced *kou*."

"So *kou* means school?" asked Arisu.

"Well, in a way it does, but you won't often see it on its own. If we want to say school we say…"

"Gaku-kou?" said *Kō*.

"It is made up of *gaku* and *kou*, but gaku-kou sounds a bit awkward, doesn't it? So we do something called small-tsu-hooking."

"Is that like ten-ten-hooking?" asked Arisu.

"Yes, very similar. It usually happens when we join two kanji together and one ends with a sharp sound and the other begins with one. We take the sharp sound off the first kanji and replace it with a small *tsu*.

"So,

gaku-kou becomes

gakkou. Which is easier to say and more elegant, don't you think?

ALICE IN KANJI LAND

"And now it is time to…"

Just then Sensei was interrupted by a lot of noise from outside the schoolhouse.

"What *is* going on?" she asked.

Everyone rushed to the windows. Outside were two pairs of Free Radical human legs, just like the pair that *Ichi*, *Ni* and *San* caught to help *Yon*. They had built a pile of earth, stuck a stick in the top of it, and now they were racing around it like crazy, yelling:

"I'm in front!"

"No, *I'm* in front!"

Because they were running in a circle around the pile of earth there was really no way of telling who was in front.

"Stop!" cried Mimi-sensei in her most teacherly voice, and the whole scene froze into a single kanji.

The earth and the stick and the human legs joined seamlessly together.

"What is that kanji, Sensei?" asked Arisu.

"It means in front or before," said Mimi-sensei. "It is pronounced *saki* on its own, but its glue-name is *sen* and that's the one we will be looking at today."

"Because a *sen*try is someone who stands *in front* of a palace?" asked *Ko*.

"It could be that," said Sensei. "If we put it together with another kanji we have learned today, we can make…"

KIN-KON-KAN-KON

"*Sen-sei...*" said Arisu. "*Sensei!*"

"That is right. Someone who was born before us and can teach us the way. It is also the *sen* in *senpai*. Again someone who has gone before us and can help us. So it may be best to think of the *sen* sound as meaning *sen*-ior, though it can mean *before* in other senses too."

"Oh my, the kanji just fit together like building bricks and make all kinds of words, don't they?"

"Yes, they do," said Mimi-sensei. "Before we end the class, we will learn one more kanji and I will show you how to make your first three-kanji word. In fact, lots of them, very easily!

"Here is the kanji."

"It looks like a mirror-five on a stick," said *Ko*.

"Yes, and holding a pencil," said Sensei. "I see this as my younger sister. She is five years old and you can't go to *Shougaku* until you are six. So here she is standing on stilts to make herself taller and holding a pencil, looking in the mirror and pretending to be a schoolgirl already."

"What she needs is another year!" said *Ko*.

"Yes, and that's what the kanji means. Year. The regular name is *Toshi*. But once again we are going to be using the glue-name today. And that is *Nen*.

"So let's try our first three-kanji word. What do you think this is?"

"*Ichi-nen-sei?*" suggested Arisu.

"Quite right," said Mimi-sensei. "And do you remember how *sei* was used for a student in

gakusei?"

"Oh! Oh! Does it mean first-year student?" asked *Ko*.

"That's exactly what it means. So there is your first three-kanji word. And as you see, you get lots of others as a free gift! *Ninensei, san'nensei,* right up to *rokunensei,* which is as high as we go in *shougaku.*"

"And that's what we are learning now, isn't it?" said Arisu. "The *ichinensei* kanji."

"*Sou desu ne,*" said Mimi-sensei.

9

Down by the Riverside

"*Yoku ganbatta minasan*. You all did very well in that rather long lesson," said Mimi-sensei. "So now we are going to have a special treat. We are going out!"

Everybody cheered and shouted "*Yatta!*" as they headed out into the sunny countryside outside the school.

They walked a few minutes until they came to a wide blue river. The river looked like this:

"Obviously a river has three things. A left bank, a right bank, and water in the middle. So this is how we write river," said Mimi-sensei.

The river giggled in a high-pitched cute voice. "How lovely to see all you kawaii children and kawaii kawaii Rabbit-sensei."

"My name is Mimi," said Sensei.

"Mimi-sensei, of course. Such *kawaii mimi*—cute ears!"

"Why, thank you," said Mimi-sensei, stroking her ears rather proudly. "You are kawaii too, *Kawa*-san."

"Kawaii, kawaii," shouted the children.

"This is *Kawa*, the river. She is called *Kawa* because like all rivers she is very, very *kawaii*."

"Wasn't there a movie called *The Bridge on the River Kawaii?*" asked Arisu. Nobody seemed to notice, and Arisu felt relieved as it seemed a silly thing to say the minute it came out of her mouth.

"*Kawa-san, yoroshiku onegaishimasu*," shouted all the children, making their politest bow.

Kawa giggled in the most kawaii manner imaginable. "*Yoroshiku ne, kawaii minasan!* You are all so kawaii that I would like you to meet my kawaii friend *Hana*-san."

Hana was a pretty flower. She looked like this:

"My name is *Hana*," said the flower.

"Hannah?" said Arisu.

"Well, there isn't an extra n, or an h on the end, but since you won't pronounce either it doesn't really matter if you put them there. English is such an odd language," said Mimi-sensei. "But be careful. *Hana* is also the name for nose."

Hana giggled. "Well, that is because I smell so sweet that everyone puts her nose near me."

And everyone did. *Hana* smelled even sweeter than she looked. Everyone started laughing and picking their own *Hana* and chattering to them.

"*Minasan!*" shouted Mimi-sensei in her best sensei-voice. "Let us look more carefully at our flowers. Please notice that *Hana* has three parts, none of which you have seen before. Pay close attention to each of them, because you will be meeting all of them very often in the future.

"The top one is

This is the grass or plant Free Radical. Its proper name is *kusa-kanmuri*, but you don't need to worry about that. I often think of it as a rose lying on top of a kanji, because it always does lie on the top. And it usually means that the kanji underneath is something plant-y.

"The next one is

This is a variant form of

So it is a *person* standing at the side of the *kanji*.

"And the last one is

This one looks a little like *Nana* (7), doesn't it? But notice that the horizontal stroke does *not* pass through the vertical line, unlike dear *Nana*. What she actually is is a spoon. Think of her as one of those plastic spoons made for tiny babies with a little lifty lid over the part where the food is to help it not spill.

"So how do these three make a flower? We need to know one more thing to understand that. If we combine the side-person (*hitoben*) and spoon (*saji*) Free Radicals, we get

化

And this means change or transform—morph, if you like. You might know the word *obake:*

お化け

It means a ghost or monster. Literally, a changed or changing thing. Sometimes an ordinary thing transformed into something strange. The *o* is honorific, just as in *o-Hi-sama*. Because no one wants to offend an *obake*.

"So why does a person with a spoon mean change? Well, I am sure you have heard of someone *stirring things up*. That means creating change. Making things different from how they were before.

"And, finally, why does

Hana mean flower? You can now see that it means grass-change. A flower is green and simple like grass when it is first born. But unlike grass, it changes as it grows. It changes from a simple green thing to a wonderful, complex creature in beautiful colors."

"Ooh! That is so lovely," said Arisu.

Hana was smiling shyly at the description of how special she is.

"Can you make two-kanji words too, *Hana*-san?" asked *Ko*.

"Indeed I can," said *Hana*. "How about some fireworks?"

The children all applauded.

"This is *Hanabi*, Flower-Fire, or fireworks. Notice that it is made of *Hana* and *Hi*, but that

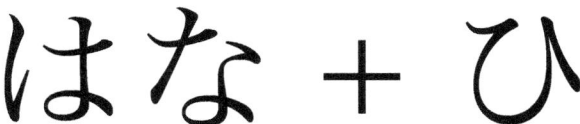

Hana + *Hi* becomes

Hana-bi because of our old friend ten-ten hooking."

As she was speaking, the sky became darker and a large drop of water splashed onto Arisu's hand. More drops followed, and then rain started hissing down.

"Oh dear, I suppose we will have to end our lovely outing," said Arisu.

"Perhaps not," said Mimi-sensei. "*Ame*-kun! *Ame*! Come here, please!"

A large kanji came floating toward them. It looked like this:

"So *that's* where rain comes from!" said Arisu.

"That's right," said Mimi-sensei. "A great big double pump with a two-handed pump-handle at the top that sends drops of rain down both channels."

"That's me!" said the kanji. "Ah'm *Ame*, the rain. They call me *Ame* because *Ah may* rain and *Ah may* not."

"Ah—I mean I—thought *ame* was a French soul," said Arisu.

"Ah sure got a French soul," said *Ame*. "Pure Cajun, ma'am. Pure Cajun."

"I have heard that Cajuns are the kindest people on earth," said Mimi-sensei.

"Never a truer word spoken, ma'am," said *Ame*.

"I wonder if you would be so terribly kind as to stop raining, so that these dear children can enjoy their educational outing."

"Shucks, ma'am, you sure got a way about you. Okay, it's a done deal." And even more quickly than it had started, the rain stopped and *o-Hi-sama* came out again.

The children laughed and danced in the sunshine, happy that their afternoon out was not rained off after all.

"*Minasan*," said Mimi-sensei. "Let's not forget that this is a school field trip."

She picked something up from the grass. "Now what do you think *this* is?" she asked.

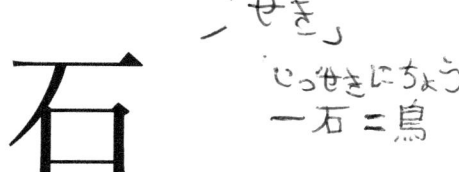

"It looks rather like *Migi*—right," said Arisu.

"Now how could I pick up *right*?" asked Mimi-sensei. "Or *left*, come to that?"

"I suppose you couldn't," admitted Arisu, though really people seemed to do a lot of things in Kanji Land that she wouldn't have thought possible.

"Let's put the two together and compare them," said Mimi-sensei.

"Oh, I see. With *Migi*, the vertical line pokes out of the top."

"Yes, that is the Hand of Friendship, if you remember. *Migi*, *Hidari* and *Tomo(dachi)* all have that same Hand of Friendship, don't they?"

"This is *Ishi*. She is a stone."

"Isn't that *Kuchi*-chan?" asked *Ko*.

"Yes, it is. She is a mouth, of course, but she is also an actress. She can play boxes and other square things. And even round things because squares can be rounds in Kanji Land. Or rather rounds are squares."

Kuchi giggled, trying to look as stone-like as possible. She didn't look *very* stone-like though, Arisu thought.

"Is she *really* a stone?"

"That's what everyone asks," said Mimi-sensei. "*Is she* really a stone? That's how stones got their name, in fact. *Is-she?*—*ishi.*"

"I see," said Arisu, though she wasn't sure she did see.

"How are we supposed to know she is a stone?" asked *Ko*-chan.

"Props," said Mimi-sensei. "All the best actresses have props. If you try to drive a nail into a round stone, what happens?"

"Why, it bends and slides off," said Arisu. "Stones are too hard to drive a nail into."

"Exactly. And this kanji shows a stone"—*Kuchi*-chan giggled again—"and a nail bending and sliding off it. That way we can be sure it is a stone and not, say, a mouth. You can see that isn't the Hand of Friendship because it has a flat top. It is a nail."

Mimi-sensei put the stone back down. "Let's see if anyone else can find something interesting to show and tell."

"I found this by the riverside," squeaked a tiny kanji. "I'm not sure what it is…"

"Why, that's an eye," said *Ko*.

"Well, it *has* an eye," said Mimi-sensei.

"But it also has legs," said the tiny kanji.

"They don't look like the legs we've seen running around before," said Arisu.

"That's right," said Mimi-sensei. "Those were Human Legs. Very mischievous. These are Animal Legs. As you see, they are smaller and more symmetrical. Not nearly as crazy-looking."

"But—an eye on animal legs…" said Arisu. "What on earth is that?"

"On earth, probably nothing," said Mimi-sensei. "But in Kanji Land it is a seashell. You often see them wandering around the shore looking at everything."

"But this isn't the seashore," said Arisu.

"They can come up river too. In their kayaks."

"Kayaks?"

"Yes. Kayaks are little boats used by *Kai*. Didn't you know that?"

"I'm afraid not. I don't even know what *Kai* are."

"These are *Kai*, of course. Seashells. As a matter of fact, you don't see them on their own all that much, but they are often inside other kanji. You'll be meeting a lot of them later in your kanji journey.

"Now before we end this lesson, let's try something new. We know how to combine one kanji with another. Now let's try combining the *same* kanji to make a different kanji."

"Combining the same kanji?" said Arisu.

"Yes. There are lots of trees here, so let's use them. You all know this kanji:

"That's *Ki*, a tree," said *Ko*.

"Quite right," said Mimi-sensei. "Now let's put two of them together."

"Oh, does it mean twin trees?" asked the tiny kanji, who seemed to be getting bolder and bolder.

"Bigger than that," said Mimi-sensei. "Does anyone else want to try?"

"A forest?" suggested Arisu.

"Not as big as that," said Mimi-sensei. "Not yet. This is a wood or copse. What do you think we call the copse?"

"When there's been a robbery?" said the tiny kanji.

"That's not *what* you call the copse," said *Ko*. "That's *when* you call the cops."

The tiny kanji blushed at her mistake.

"It is called *hayashi*," said Mimi-sensei, "because the little wood or copse is a *high-ashy* place—full of high ash trees."

"So it's not the *ashi* that are legs," said *Ko*.

"No, it's *hayashi*. But you would need very *high ashi* to be tall enough to see over the trees.

"Now let's go one step further."

"*That's* a forest, I think," said Arisu.

"So it is," said Mimi-sensei. "And it is called *mori*, because it has even *more* trees than *hayashi*.

"The field trip is over," said Mimi-sensei. "You all did very well. You may now go home."

But of course Arisu didn't know where to go.

10

The Owl That Went *Pfam!*

The children ran off in different directions, and Arisu found herself alone. The great square shining sun was halfway down the western sky. It was still a glorious afternoon, but Arisu realized that evening would come and that, unlike the children and Mimi-sensei, she had no home to go to.

She had no idea how to leave Kanji Land, but she really had no place *in* Kanji Land. Should she go back the way she came and hope to meet *Juu* again? *Juu* was probably somewhere else by now.

Suddenly she felt tired. She saw a big, leafy, inviting tree and sat down under it.

"I think I'll take a little rest," she said to herself.

As she did there was a flash of light, and a kanji appeared with a loud *pfam!*

"Oh! What was that?" cried Arisu loudly, for she was very much startled.

No one answered.

"How curious," said Arisu to herself. "I have the strangest feeling that I am being watched."

There was another *pfam!* and another kanji appeared.

Arisu stood up in alarm. Yet another flash and another kanji *pfam!ed* into being.

"What is going on?" cried Arisu. "Why are these kanji appearing out of nowhere?"

There was silence. And then the sound of a drawn-out yawn.

"It isn't nowhere," said a voice.

"What isn't nowhere?" asked Arisu.

"Where the kanji are coming from. They aren't coming from nowhere. They're coming from *you*."

"From me?"

The voice yawned again. "This is Kanji Land," it said.

"I know that," said Arisu.

"In Kanji Land," said the voice, as if it were explaining something to a very, very small child, "nothing can happen without a kanji. You keep doing things, so obviously you keep invoking kanji."

"I haven't been doing anything," said Arisu.

"Of course you have. First you had a rest.

So naturally the *rest* kanji had to appear."

"It's a tree," said Arisu.

"Not just a tree," said the voice. "There is someone beside the tree."

THE OWL THAT WENT *PEAM!*

"Someone? Who?"

"It could be anyone. But as it happens, it's you."

"You are speaking in riddles. What do you mean?"

The voice yawned again.

"The kanji is a person by a tree. Obviously a person by a tree is going to have a *rest*. In this case, the person was you."

"I see. So how do you say 'rest' in Japanese?"

"*Yasumi*. You might have heard people say *o-yasumi nasai*. That is a very polite way of saying 'have a rest'."

"*Yasumi*. What a curious word."

"Legend has it that the first people just ran around all the time and never rested. Then finally one of them got tired and went and sat under a tree. The others said, 'You can't do that!'"

"But the person under the tree just said, '*Ya! Sue me!*' and went on resting.

"A very unrefined person if you ask me. Probably a human."

"What are you?"

"The wisest of the wise," replied the voice. And a large white bird with huge eyes swooped down from the branches of the tree.

"My name is Hukurou."

"Hook-a-row?" said Arisu. Looking closely, it *did* seem that the bird was crocheted.

"*Hu-KU-rou.*"

"Why, you're an owl."

"I have that honor."

"If everything has a kanji, why can't I see *your* kanji?"

"Elementary, my dear child."

"It isn't elementary to me."

"No, but you are. First-year Elementary. So obviously you can't see *my* kanji."

"What were those other kanji? I admit I had a rest, but I didn't do anything else."

"Of course you did," said Hukurou. "You said you had a feeling you were being watched. And you were. I was watching you. Wondering what noisy person had disturbed my sleep. Anyway, when you said that, naturally the *watching* kanji had to appear.

"Why, that's a seashell."

"No, it isn't. A seashell is an eye with *animal legs*:

"Watching or looking has *human legs*. The kind that run around all over the place staring at things. Like humans. Don't mix them up and they won't mix you up."

"How do you say 'look'?" asked Arisu.

見る

"*Miru*. As in 'look in the *miru*'. You can put *mi(ru)* together with other kanji you know to make other words. For example:

Hana-mi."

"Flower-see?"

"Yes. *Hanami* is when the *sakura* (cherry blossom) comes in spring and everyone goes out into the park with food and drink to look at the lovely tree-flowers. Sitting under the trees, just as you were when I heard you."

"Hmm. Well, I did rest, and I did say I was being watched. But that was all I did. I certainly didn't do anything after that."

"Yes, you did. You stood up.

立

This is the *standing-up* kanji."

"It's that top hat again."

"It gets around, doesn't it? This time it's sitting on top of a vase to look as if it's *standing up* all by itself."

"How is 'stand up' said?"

"*Tatsu.*"

"Ah. The kanji *kind of* looks like a T and an A upside down, doesn't it?" said Arisu. "And then the *tsu* makes it *tatsu.*"

"Hm," said Hukurou unconvincedly. "The bar of the A has slipped to the top."

"Of course. That's because it's upside down," said Arisu.

"Are you sure you're human?" asked Hukurou. "You talk just like a Kanji Lander sometimes."

"Good heavens, I suppose I'm picking it up," said Arisu.

"I suppose you are." There was a *pfam!* and another kanji appeared.

"Oh, that startled me!" cried Arisu. "What is that?"

"Heaven," said Hukurou.

"Heaven?"

"Yes. You said 'good heavens'. So naturally heaven popped up."

"Is that what heaven looks like?"

"From here, yes. It's the *one big* thing above us."

"Oh, I see. *Dai* with *Ichi* above. How is it said?"

"*Ten,*" said Hukurou.

"*Ten* eleven rhymes with heaven."

"Just *Ten*. Not eleven," said Hukurou pedantically.

"Well, you *can* see eleven in it if you stand it on its side," said Arisu.

THE OWL THAT WENT *PFAM!*

"That settles it. You're not human," said Hukurou.

Arisu held out her hand.

"Hm. Five fingers. So I suppose... Well, your *spirit* isn't human, that's for sure."

Pfam!

"What's *that*?" asked Arisu.

"It's complicated," said Hukurou.

"It certainly is," said Arisu.

"It's spirit," said Hukurou.

"My spirit?" asked Arisu.

"Anyone's spirit. Not just people either. Let's look at something simpler first."

"Oh yes, let's," said Arisu.

"This is steam or vapor. You can see it rising into the air and puff-puffing in three puffy-puffs.

"Now with the X at the bottom—well, X marks the Spot, as you know. And in this case the Spot is you or me or anything, and the vapor is the invisible, untouchable essence of us. The spirit."

"I see..."

"Both of them are pronounced *ki*."

"Like tree?"

"Yes. Didn't you ever hear of tree-spirits? And when you look at it, you see that it is a bit like the *ki* hiragana."

"Oh yes, the open bit at the bottom and the lines at the top."
"If we put *ki* together with the last kanji we get…"

"*Ten-ki?*" asked Arisu.
"Yes, *tenki*."
"*Heaven-Spirit?*"
"Exactly that. The spirit or mood of heaven. In other words, the weather."
"So when heaven is in a good mood, it's sunny?"
"Yes."
"But where are all these kanji coming *from?*" asked Arisu.
Pfam!

"A tree?"
"Not a tree," said Hukurou. "See the horizontal line toward the bottom?"
"Yes."

"That represents the ground. What is important about this kanji is what comes below that line. The Root, the Source, the Origin."

"So this is the Source of all the kanji?"

"The Source of everything. And since everything is a kanji in Kanji Land, certainly the source of the kanji."

"The more I look at it, the more it looks like a book."

"It is a book too, of course. And just to round things out—heh heh—it is the counter for long round things, like pencils or bottles or fingers.

"Whatever it is doing, it is generally pronounced *hon*."

"So *hon* is a book…"

"Yes."

"And the root or source of things…"

"Yes."

"And the counter for long round things?"

"Yes. For example:

biiru ni-hon is two long round things of beer. That is to say, two bottles of beer."

"How confusing. All those meanings."

"If we start at the root, it all makes sense. Root is the *root* meaning. Do you understand that?"

"Yes."

"The taproot of a tree is long and round. Hence the secondary meaning of long, round things."

"But what about books?"

"They were long and round too. Originally books were scrolls. Only more recently did they become flat things with hinged pages."

"I *see!*"

"Now if we put *hon* together with a kanji we already know, we can get

Nihon. The place where the sun rises. Thus the origin of the sun. *Nihon*, Japan."

"So *o-Hi-sama* can be *Ni*?"

"*Hi* can be *Nichi*. This shortening to *Ni* is a special case."

"And it *does* look like a book now," said Arisu. "I guess it's the Book of all the kanji in the world."

She peeped inside.

"Don't open it!" cried Hukurou, but too late. Something shot barking out of the book, followed by something buzzing. Hukurou pushed the book shut quickly.

"If you open that, who knows what will come pouring out?"

"What did?" asked Arisu.

"This dog for a start."

"Why, that's a person throwing a stick!" said Arisu.

"Not at all. It's *Dai* with a *droplet*. I imagine the droplet is that potion that turns people into dogs. But the image of a person throwing a stick certainly makes it clearer that it is a dog."

"What's its name?"

"*Inu*."

"Why *inu*?"

THE OWL THAT WENT *PFAM!*

"Because it lives *in you* house. Unlike, say, a horse or a cow, which lives in its own house."

"And what's it chasing?"

"A bug."

"That looks like *Naka*."

"It is *Naka*. With a hammer."

"Why?"

"Because when an insect got *inside* the house back in the old days people would chase it with a hammer."

"What's it called?"

"*Mushi*. And before you say 'why' again, I'll tell you. Because if they managed to hit it with the hammer it went mushy."

But Arisu was already distracted. "Look at the *mushi* fly and the *inu* run after it. They are both so *fast!*"

Pfam!

"Why, it's *Juu* with the sun on her head!"

"Or the great Flower of Morning."

"What does it mean?"

"Early, or fast."

"Is fast the same as early?"

"Of course. The faster you run the earlier you arrive."

"And nothing rises *earlier* than the Great Flower of Morning."

"Exactly. And have you ever seen the sun move so fast through the sky that there seem to be *ten* of it?"

"How is it said?"

"We usually say

hayai."

"*Hayai*. I wonder why?"

"When you move really fast you have to keep a *high eye* all the time. Look down for a second and you crash into something."

"*Naruhodo*," said Arisu.

"And now if you'll excuse me, I will go back to my *yasumi*."

"*O-yasumi nasai*," said Arisu and sat down on the grass because there seemed nothing much else to do.

Pfam!

"And I'd appreciate it if you'd stop *pfam!ing*," said Hukurou, a little testily.

"*I'm* not *pfam!ing*," said Arisu. "And anyway why does the same kanji *pfam!* twice? We've already had *hayai*."

"That isn't *hayai*," said Hukurou. "Can't you see the plant Free Radical on the top? That tells us it's some kind of plant."

"A fast plant?"

"An early plant. The first and simplest plant in the world that grows before anything else."

THE OWL THAT WENT *PFAM!*

"Grass?" asked Arisu.

"Grass," said Hukurou. "Or *kusa* to give it its proper name. Because *kus are* always eating it."

"*Kus?*"

"Cows. Scots or German. I'm tired. It's the best I can do. *Oyasumi.*"

"What a grumpy owl," thought Arisu. Hukurou disappeared and Arisu wondered what to do now.

11

The Car That Drove Herself

Arisu sat on the grass watching the *inu* and the *mushi* bark and buzz noisily off into the distance.

She tried saying and doing a number of things, but nothing went *pfam!*

"I'm sure that owl was responsible for all the *pfam!ing*," she thought.

O-Hi-sama was getting lower and lower in the western sky. Arisu wondered what she should do for the night. Maybe she could sleep right here. It was warm enough. At least it was now. And it wasn't raining. At least for the present. And what else could she do?

Then she heard a rumbling sound. Something was coming along the road.

As it came nearer she could see that it was a car of sorts. It had a big axle through the middle, two big wheels at the sides and its body was shining like the sun:

As it came closer Arisu could see that it had big headlamps with long eyelashes.

The car blinked her eyelashes and stopped.

"*Daijoubu?*" she said. "Are you all right?"

Arisu looked dazedly at the talking car and said nothing.

"My name is *Kuru-ma*," said the car. Arisu thought vaguely about *o-kaa-san*, the mother who drove children in the car. Was *Kuru-ma* a car who was a mother?

"*Kuru-ma*..." said Arisu.

THE CAR THAT DROVE HERSELF

"I always *kuru* when someone needs me," she explained.

"*Kuru...*" said Arisu.

"Yes, *kuru*." *Kuruma* projected the kanji onto her windshield.

"It means *come*. That's what I do. I come."

"Why does that mean come?" asked Arisu.

"Well, it's a bit of a tale, but I'll tell you if you like," said *Kuruma*.

"Yes, please," said Arisu, who was glad of the pleasant company.

"You know what a tree looks like?"

"Yes."

"Some trees grow rice. And when they do you can see the rice grains in the branches:

So that's rice. It's called *kome*. I suppose because the rice grains look like little eyes: *ko-me*."

"Oh! My first all-Japanese mnemonic! But rice doesn't grow on trees. It grows in very wet fields."

"These days it does. But things were more convenient in the old days. Rice grew on trees. Not just that, but you didn't need to harvest it. It came by itself."

"Did it?"

"It certainly did. You called it to come with the magical cry *ku-ru! ku-ru!* And every bit of rice would put on its top hat...

and *come* along by itself."

"Like calling the *kus* in."

"*Kus?*" said *Kuruma*.

"Just something an owl said."

"Not that *pfam!ing* bird?"

"So the owl *is* the *pfam!er*."

"I don't think it's intentional, but *pfam!s* certainly go off more than normal whenever it's around.

"Anyway, it's nearly evening and…"

Pfam!

"Is that owl around here?"

"I think it's over in that tree," said Arisu.

"That kanji is evening, anyway. It's a cousin of

Tsuki, the moon. This one is a crescent moon, as you see."

THE CAR THAT DROVE HERSELF

"It looks rather like katakana TA to me."

"That's because everyone says *TAdaima* when they *kuru* home in the evening."

"Is it said *ta*?"

"No. It's mostly said *yuu*. Because evening is when *yuu* come home."

"It is evening too, isn't it?" said Arisu. "*O-Hi-sama* looks so large and golden-red and—uh—square."

"Yes, beautiful," said *Kuruma*. "That's what we call

Yuu-hi, the evening sun."

"*Yuuhi*," said Arisu. "What a lovely name!"

"Speaking of which, what is yours?" asked *Kuruma*.

"My what?"

"*Na. Na-mae...*"

"Oh, that's *Yuu* with *Kuchi*."

"That's right. When one approached the city at night, the gatekeepers asked 'Who goes there?' and one had to say one's name (with one's mouth, of course)."

"So that is name?"

"Yes. It's said *na*, but we often don't use it on its own. If I mean someone's name, I talk about the name on their front."

"Like those name tags people wear on their front at conferences?"

"Yes. This is *mae*, front…"

"That's *Tsuki*, moon, on the left, isn't it?"

"Yes, in her in-kanji form

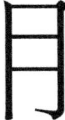

and on the right is

which is an in-kanji form of

THE CAR THAT DROVE HERSELF

Katana. The sword."

"And what are those two things at the top?"

"Those are very interesting. They get called horns sometimes, but they are certainly not devil-horns. They are more like a sacred glow, I think, because they tend to mark something that is right and good. Sometimes they are supported by *Ichi*, as they are here, and sometimes they sit by themselves. I call them the Glow of Correctness or of Ceremony."

"It does have a very correct and ceremonious glow, doesn't it—that shiny top?"

"It does."

"But the whole kanji is quite a complicated picture," said Arisu.

"Not too complicated now you know the parts. What it shows is an ancient *ceremony* held in the *moonlight* in which a *sword* is carried at the *front* of the procession. Naturally it means *front*.

"So let's look at your *name-in-front* now. It's easiest to remember the pronunciation all together."

na-mae. As you see, it is very easy because it is just like 'name' with an extra *a* just before the end."

"*Namae*. I like it. There are two moons in it, aren't there?"

"There are. But what *is* it?"

"Hmm. Well, a Moon and a Mouth and then a Glow of Ceremony, another Moon and a Sword."

"That's not what I meant. I meant, what is your *namae*?"

"Oh!" Arisu bowed very courteously. "*Watashi wa Arisu desu. Yoroshiku onegaishimasu.*"

"*Yoroshiku ne*. What a very proper little girl."

Pfam!

"Oh, what's that?"

"That is *proper*. Right. Correct. Straightforward. Do you remember that our friend

Tom means stop? Well, the new kanji means *stopping at the line*. Keeping within bounds. Being correct and proper. We use it in words like

tadashii. Which is what I was calling you. Very proper.

"That's why the kanji *pfam!ed* up."

"Is that because when you have been very proper you feel pretty pleased with yourself and shout *Tadaa*!"

"Well, if you do it aloud it rather spoils the effect of being *tadashii*. But most of us have a little quiet *Tadaa!* about it. Of course, you could be shouting *Tada*-ima, I have returned to the Right Path!"

"Why is there a *shii* on the end?"

"Now that's interesting. A lot of adjectives have *shii* on the end. It's like a longer form of that *i* that turns something into an adjective. So *tada-shii* means that *something* is correct, just as *aka-i* means that *something* is red."

"Is there a difference between *shii* and *i*?"

"Yes, there is. *Shii*-adjectives tend to be about human-things and feeling-things. *I*-words are things like *red* or *blue*, *big* or *small*—you know all those, don't you?—They are definite things. Something is either red or it isn't. *Shii*-words are things like *correct* and *beautiful*, *sad* and *happy*, things we feel. Things that can't be measured or proved but that belong to our hearts."

"Oh, that is interesting."

"You don't need to 'learn' that. It isn't a learny sort of thing. But it is very well worth knowing.

"Anyway, let's get away from here. All that noisy *pfam!ing* noise gets on my nerves."

Pfam!

"What's that?"

"More noise."

"No, I mean what's the kanji?"

"Noise, sound. That's what it is."

"*Stand* on the *sun*? That's *sound*?"

"It really is. You can imagine it with these *pfam!ers*, can't you? They would even stand on the sun making noise across the whole world."

"I think of a beautiful singer standing on the sun singing radiant music," said Arisu.

"What a pretty thought. The kanji is pronounced *Oto*."

"Like Otto and Co. *Otoko*."

"Well, men do make a lot of noise sometimes. The glue-name is *Ne*."

"*Neigh*? Men and horses both make noise!"

"So they do. But it's getting late, so why don't I drive you home, Arisu-chan?"

"That's—a bit of a problem."

"A problem?"

"I—I don't really have a home."

"A homeless child?"

"Well, no. But I don't have a home in Kanji Land. I'm not from here. I'm—human."

"Really? May I see your hands?"

Arisu put out her hands.

"*Ara ara!* Five fingers. I've never seen that before! How remarkable. You'll need to stay somewhere for the night, though. Get in and we'll see what we can find."

Kuruma opened her driver's seat door.

"I—can't drive," said Arisu.

"Oh, don't worry about that. I drive myself. I'm a self-drive *kuruma*."

It was wonderful fun to drive all alone in a car and yet have someone to talk to.

"What are all those tall thin trees?" asked Arisu.

THE CAR THAT DROVE HERSELF

"*Take*," said *Kuruma*.

"I can't take one unless we stop. And they are a bit big to take anyway."

"Not 'take', *ta-ke*. Bamboo."

"*Take*-ing someone in is the same as *bamboo*zling her," said Arisu.

"As you see, there are two of them, tall and thin, with branches widening at the top and drooping down. Bamboo is like that. It goes up a long, thin way before there are any leaves or branches."

"There are a lot more than two here, aren't there?"

"Yes. This is a

chiku-rin. A bamboo thicket. *Chiku* is *take*'s glue-name."

"That second kanji is *hayashi*, isn't it? What we call the copse."

"That's right. A small forest. Its glue-name is *rin*. You can think of it as a *ring* of bamboo trees."

Arisu enjoyed the tall elegance and cool green of the bamboo trees. Soon they saw some houses in the distance.

"We are coming to the village," said *Kuruma*.

"It looks like more trees."

"It is a tree and something else."

"What else?"

"An inch—which stands for measurement in general. It's one of those things where you move the horizontal part up and down the vertical to get the exact measure of something. The little part is the inch itself."

"This may be a silly question, but how is it a village?"

"Before people start building a village, the area is forest. They have to clear some trees so they have land for fields. Cut some trees to build houses. Keep other trees for apples and prettiness. But the first thing they have to do is come and measure the trees and work out what they are going to do.

"So *tree-measuring* is the first step in making a village."

"What is the last step?" asked Arisu.

"When everything is built, someone paints a beautiful mural on the walls. That is the very last step. Then the village is finished and one can call it a *mura*—a village."

"Does *mura* really come from mural?" asked Arisu.

"No, the other way around. After all, parental means what parents do or have. Mural means what a *mura* has."

As they drove through the village, the sky was still a radiant blue, even as the *o-Hi-sama* sank lower.

"What a lovely sky," said *Kuruma*.

"Is that the sky?"

"It is."

"It isn't wearing a hat, is it?"

"No. That Free Radical on top is a House or Roof:

"You see, unlike the Top Hat, it is enclosing at the sides. A protecting roof with a chimney on top."

"And Human Legs under that. And Craft or Making."

"That's right. Humans—and others—run around. They build their villages and paint their pictures and do all the things they do. And over it all—no matter where we run or what we make—is that Great Roof we call the sky."

"How do we say 'sky'?"

"*Sora*. After all, you can't *soar* anywhere but the sky, can you?"

"And it is still so blue."

"Yes, it is still

ao-zora. Blue sky. You know *ao* already, I believe. And *sora* becomes *zora* because…"

"I know, I know!" cried Arisu excitedly. "Ten-ten hooking!"

"All right. Now we're coming into town."

"It's a field and…"

"That thing next to the field is often seen as a nail, and you could say that people come to the fields and hammer and nail until they've built a town.

"However, in this kanji I see it as a street lamp. You could say that when a country area gets street lamps, it is turning into a town.

"You could go even further and see the field in this case as a very simplified map of a town with just four blocks and two roads running between them—and a street lamp, of course. That is how country areas turn into towns."

"How do we say 'town'?" asked Arisu.

"*Machi*. You know, there are very few fairy tales set in a modern-ish city with street lamps and such. In fact, I can only think of one…"

"The Little *Match*-Girl," said Arisu. "But that's a sad story."

"It is," agreed *Kuruma*.

"I think of a *machi* as different from a *mura*, where all the houses are higgledy-piggledy. In a *machi*, all the houses are in *matching* rows."

"Yes, you are very right, Arisu-chan. And now we're here."

"Where?" asked Arisu.

"*Here*," said *Kuruma*.

12

The Doll at the Crossroads

Kuruma braked herself and opened her driver-side door. Arisu took this as a hint to get out and did so.

"I can't come into the house with you," said *Kuruma*. "*Kuruma* don't go into houses, you know."

"No, of course not."

"Now you'll need this…"

Kuruma handed Arisu a coin.

"That's *en*, a circle. In English it gets called *yen*. But it isn't. It's just *en*."

"It looks like two flags facing each other."

"Even when Japan was split into two parts, each with its own flag, you could spend your *en* in either."

"Are you sure it's all right for me to have this?"

"It isn't worth much at all. But you need it. Purely symbolic really."

"I… see."

"Now, here's what you have to do. You have go down that little side street and find the Thread…"

"The thread?"

"Yes, it's a thread or piece of string. It looks like this…"

"It's small at the bottom."

"That's right. The bottom is a form of *Shou*. But the top you'll just have to memorize. This is your Thread of Destiny, you see. It's called *ito* because every *hito* has a Thread of Destiny. At least until she stops breathing (*h* is a breath). Of course, the kanji itself can be any thread or string, or even knitting yarn."

"But this is my—Thread of Destiny."

"Yes. Follow the thread until you come to a house marked

Mo-ji."

"*Moji?*"

"Yes. It means letters or characters. Everything here in Kanji Land is made up of *Moji*. What can you tell me about the *Moji* that make up *Moji?*"

"Hmm… There's that top hat again."

"Yes. Gentlemen in black top hats—as well as ladies in cute colored ones—exchange letters and poems. There is the criss-cross of exchange underneath the hat.

This means literature or it can mean a sentence or literary style. It is the very essence of written language. The *exchange* of educated people (in *top hats*).

"And the other one?"

Arisu answered, "Why, it's just like

Gaku. Only the crown is simpler."

"That's right. *Gaku* is the child with the Shining Crown of Learning. This one is the single, basic element of that learning. One letter or character. One kanji or one kana.

"If you look at the elements, it is a child in a house. A single child of the house of learning. One character."

"So *Moji* is one character from the great world of written language."

"That's right. You are going to the House of *Moji*. Goodbye and good luck."

"Goodbye, *Kuruma*-san. Thank you for everything."
Kuruma revved her engine and drove away with a merry beep-beep.

Arisu walked hesitantly down the little side street that *Kuruma* had indicated. She saw the thread lying in the road and started to follow it until she came to the house with a large wooden sign with *Moji* in golden kanji.

She knocked at the door, but nobody answered.

She knocked again and the door creaked open.

She looked inside. She saw a very neat room, and yet it seemed somehow unreal. Like a dollhouse. A doll was seated in one of the chairs, but there seemed to be no one at home.

"Ah, come in," said a voice.

Arisu stepped inside.

"You're a little early. Do you have the *en*?"

Arisu realized that the doll was talking. She walked nervously over to her and held out the coin that *Kuruma* had given her.

"Thank you, thank you."

"*Watashi wa*…"

"Arisu *desu*. Yes, I know."

"You know?"

"Of course I know. I'm The Doll. Congratulations."

"On what?"

"On finishing the First Year kanji, of course. You have, you know. Well, not *quite*. Would you mind picking me up and putting me on that table over there by the big crystal ball?"

Arisu carefully picked up The Doll and took it over to the table. On the table was

THE DOLL AT THE CROSSROADS

"It's like the *Ou*, the monarch, isn't it? But you see that one droplet the monarch is holding. That's the Great Jewel or the Great Orb. A sphere or gem. It is called *Tama*."

"Because it sits on the TAble and it's MAgic."

"Yes. Rather important magic. For one thing, I could use it to send you back to the place from whence you came."

"Oh…"

"You've finished, you see. Graduated, as it were. Now you know all the First Year kanji."

"I thought I was just having an adventure."

"That's the best way to learn. But now you've finished the adventure. So we could wake you up."

"Was all this a dream?"

"In a way it was a dream. In another way the human world is a dream. It all depends how you look at things. So the question is, do you want to go back where you came from?"

"What happens if I don't?"

"Well, there is life beyond the First Year, you know. More adventures. More things to learn. You don't have to decide just yet. I need to write a note to the readers. Then you can let me know your decision."

"The readers?"

"Don't worry about them. You can't see them. They can see you though."

"Are they—good people?"

"I hope so. But let me write my note."

The Doll picked up a pen that was almost as big as she was and started writing:

Great power…

Interlude

With Great Power...

Dear Reader-sama,

Congratulations.
You have now learned all the First Year kanji—and several others too.
Please remember that with great power comes great responsibility and use your new-found abilities wisely, for the benefit of all sentient beings.
If you wish to learn all kanji for JLPT N5, you will need to go on into the new lands beyond this page.
If you wish to learn the kanji in Japanese school-year order, the rest of this book will give you a substantial head start on the Second Year kanji.
If you are using the Alice in Kanji Land *Anki deck, you will write them into your heart and know them whenever you see them.*
If you wish to follow Arisu on her further adventures, you have only to turn the page. The choice is yours.

Will you continue your adventure?

Press A to continue
Press B to save and quit

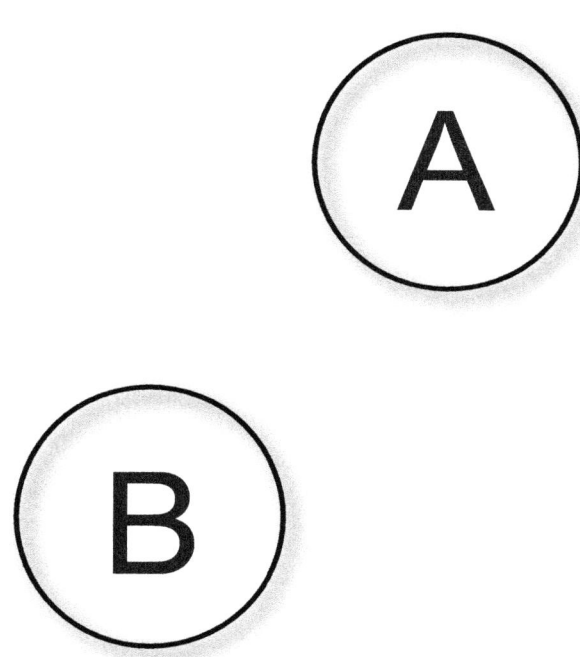

13

The Man Behind the Hats

Arisu awoke. She was in a pretty little bed in a pretty little room that she had never seen before.

There was a knock on the door.

"*Haitte*," she said, remembering what *Sen* had said when *Juu* knocked on his door.

A rabbit dressed in a maid's uniform opened the door.

"*Ohayou gozaimasu, ojou-sama*," she said.

"*Ohayou gozaimasu*," said Arisu. "It may be a silly question but—where am I?"

"In the House of *Moji*, of course," said the rabbit-maid. "You paid your *en* and stayed the night. All your hit points are restored."

"I... see."

"Is *ojou-sama* ready for her breakfast?"

"Oh yes. That would be very nice."

"Follow me please."

Arisu followed the maid to a room with several tables. She was ushered to a seat. At a nearby table sat a gentleman reading a newspaper (Arisu wondered how long it would be before she knew enough kanji to read a newspaper). He was wearing a stovepipe hat with a label on it that read:

THE MAN BEHIND THE HATS

"Why, that's…" Arisu stopped. It would not be polite to point someone out to the maid, she thought. Especially as the name she knew for him did not sound very flattering.

"Mr. Hatter," whispered the maid. "He makes those top hats you see all over the place."

Then she said aloud in her proper maid voice, "Would *ojou-sama* care to *taberu*?"

"*Taberu*?" asked Arisu.

Abruptly Mr. Hatter stood up. "Eat!" he shouted. "Fill your empty *o-Naka*! Break your fast. We call it *taberu* because we do it at the *teeberu* (table)."

"Thank you, good sir," said Arisu.

"Why, it's *Arisu*!" cried Mr. Hatter. "I'd know you anywhere."

"But I don't believe we've ever met before," said Arisu.

"True, true," said Mr. Hatter. "Never met before. Still, why let a little thing like that stand between old friends? Hmm? Why?"

"Well, I suppose…"

"And a very pretty suppose it is too. Now you want to know all about this *taberu* kanji, I imagine."

"Indeed I…"

"No need to apologize. It's not taboo, it's *taberu*. The kanji is quite a long story so you might want to do your morning exercises before we start."

Arisu wondered if she ought to do something exercise-y to humor Mr. Hatter and half stood up, but he motioned her to sit down again.

"No time for that now. It starts with clothing."

"What does?"

"You'll find out if you listen patiently.

"Clothing looks like this. Naturally it is wearing one of my hats as no outfit of clothing is complete without one. Underneath the hat are what looks rather like capital *I* and a small *t*. That is because my hats are *It*—the Very Thing. And so are any clothes that go under them.

"Clothing is said *koromo*, but we don't use that word on its own very often so you don't need to learn the pronunciation right now.

"However, these clothes are very important because they go into a lot of kanji. For example:

which means *good*. As you see, the clothes are a bit cut down, and, tragically, they have lost my hat. But I think you can see the meaning."

"White clothes?" asked Arisu.

"Prezactly. And of course in the old movies *bad* characters wore *black* clothes and *good* characters wore *white* clothes. So 'white clothes' means *good*.

"We say it

yoi, or more commonly, *ii*. You probably know that already. You won't need the kanji for it much at this stage, but it helps you with other things.

"Now imagine a roof.

"This is the *Human Roof* Free Radical."

"Why *Human* Roof?"

"Because it looks rather like a *hito*. Let's pop it on top of *good*:

And what is the most good thing you can do under a roof?"

"Eat?"

"Exisely. *Taberu*. Break your fast. Put the L in unch."

"Phew!" said Arisu. "That was complicated."

"You're not an *ichi-nen-sei* any more," said Mr. Hatter.

"Are all the new kanji that complicated?" asked Arisu worriedly.

"Oh yes. Most of them are much worse than that. They often take up a whole sheet of paper with just one kanji. Sometimes the side of a building."

"They don't," whispered the maid. "Lots of them are quite simple."

"I heard that!" said Mr. Hatter. "They get worse and worse, I tell you. You want a drink? A simple drink? *This* is what you have to go through:

Nomu. Drink. Because you go *nom-nom*."

"I thought that was eating."

"No, eating is *taberu*. Try not to get confused."

"But half of this *is taberu*, isn't it?"

"Yes. The clothes are very truncated by now. Down to a pair of truncs, you might say. But that's certainly *taberu* on the left. And on the right is a shortage or a yawn.

"That is a person constricted by a clamp. That can mean shortage, or it can mean she is *clamping* her lips to blow—or yawning, which is a bit like blowing.

"So, put that together with eating and you get drinking. Because you can just suck or yawn in your drink. You don't have to chew it like food. And if you are *constricted* and can't get food, usually you can at least drink water.

"There, that wasn't too hard, was it?"

Arisu looked a bit worried.

"Don't worry," whispered the maid. "That's about as hard as it gets. Most of it is easier."

"There's lots more to do," said Mr. Hatter. "So finish your breakfast and don't be a

nagai aida."

THE MAN BEHIND THE HATS

"What is that?" asked Arisu suspiciously. She wasn't at all sure she wanted to be called a *nagai aida*.

"Long time," said Mr. Hatter. "Don't be a long time.

is *long*. It's a book on a pile of clothes. Obviously when you get a book that's too long you throw it on a pile of clothes and say you'll read it some time or other. And you never do. It is said *nagai* because when people nag you they go on and on for a very long time."

"And the *i* is because it's an adjective."

"Yes. Now as for

That is an interval or space between two things. Often an interval of time. The kanji shows the great Sun Gates with another sun in between them. Between the Sun Gate of dawn and the Sun Gate of night is the *interval* when the sun shines *between* them. That is said *aida*.

"Just remember *nagai aida*. Because *Aida* is an opera that goes on for a very long time."

"Does it have a long interval?" asked Arisu.

"I shouldn't wonder. But we don't. We have to get to the Time Machine. And you'll need your Kanjidex."

"Kanjidex? I don't have one."

"Yes, you do. It's this little device." Mr. Hatter handed it to her. "It's been recording all your kanji as you learned them. You don't get it in your actualistic hand until now though."

"Why not?"

"They're expensive. We can't go around giving out Kanjidexes to people who won't get through the *ichinensei* kanji. You are a trusted kanji *gakusei* now."

Arisu smiled. "Thank you so much."

"Don't thank me. It's that Doll. Now finish up your breakfast and let's go. Gotta catch 'em all."

14

The Time Machine

Arisu and Mr. Hatter left the House of *Moji* and walked out into the town. It was full of kanji bustling to and fro, tall buildings, interesting-looking shops, and lots of *kuruma* and buses on the road.

"What's the kanji for 'bus'?" asked Arisu.

"There isn't one," said Mr. Hatter. "It's just BASU in katakana. There are lots of words like that."

"That's nice and easy," said Arisu.

"We are going to the Time Machine," said Mr. Hatter. "It isn't far. There *are* kanji for that, but we don't use them much. Mostly we say TAIMU MASHIN in katakana."

"Will we be going into the past or the future?"

"Going? The Time Machine isn't a vehicle. It makes time. What we are doing is what is called

Do you know what that means?"

"Um, miru-gaku?"

"Do you see a kana '*ru*' in there?"

"No…"

"Neither do I. If there isn't a kana '*ru*' or '*u*' or '*ku*' or some other *u*-row kana, then it isn't the verb. Kanji sitting alone without kana are not verbs. So it isn't *miru*. You can say that for sure."

"I can't say what it *is* though."

"*Ken*. The glue-name of *mi(ru)*. In English 'ken' means *know*. In Japanese it means *see*."

"Now I see—I mean, ken," said Arisu. "So it's *kengaku*?"

"Yes, it is."

"See-learn?"

"Indubitably. A field trip, a bit of research. Learning by looking. And here we are. You have come for an educational tour of the Time Machine. To learn all about *toki*."

"*Toki*?"

"*Toki*. Time. You know. As in 'ticky-*tocky* went the clocky'."

"Is that where the word comes from?"

"Of course. And it looks like this:

"That's *o-Hi-sama* on the left," said Arisu.

"Quite right. Do you recognize anyone else?"

"Oh yes. *Tsuchi*, earth, and that measuring-inch thing."

"Yes. Those two together make

tera, a temple. Temples belong to heaven. Heaven is what can measure earth. Thus *earth-measure*, temple. *Terra* means earth in English, of course. As in *terra firma*."

"I thought that was Latin," said Arisu.

"Latin, English, some foreign language anyway.

"Now, in the old days the temples told the time. People didn't have their own clocks. The temple rang a bell on the hour. Each time the sun had moved one full degree toward evening. So *sun+temple* means time.

THE TIME MACHINE

Ticky-*tocky* time. It also means hour. But you'll learn about that inside, I shouldn't wonder."

They were outside a large building covered in clocks. Big clocks, small clocks. Clocks in all colors. Some of them had numbers like regular clocks, but many of them had other symbols around their faces. Some had five or more hands. They seemed to tell every possible aspect of time.

On the front was a sign saying

"Well, in you go," said Mr. Hatter.

"A–aren't you coming?" asked Arisu nervously.

"Do I look like a school teacher? Well, do I?"

"Not a bit," said Arisu very truthfully.

"Just tell them I sent you and show them your Kanjidex," said Mr. Hatter. "I'll see you later. *Mata ne*. Come back to the House of *Moji* at lunch time."

"*Mata ne*," said Arisu and pushed open the big door of the Time Machine.

Inside, the walls were covered in even more clocks of every imaginable kind. As Arisu was staring dumbfounded at them all, a person in uniform rushed up to her.

"Hey, you! What are you doing in here?"

"Um—Mr. Hatter sent me."

"*Mr. Hatter*? What nonsense is he up to now? Whatever it is, you can do it somewhere else. We don't have time here."

"I thought you had nothing *but* time here," said Arisu.

"That's a different sense of 'time'."

"Oh…"

"Some people have no sense of time. Some people have several. Now, be on your way please, little girl."

"He said to show you this," said Arisu, holding out her Kanjidex.

"Ah, a *gaku-sei*. Well, why didn't you *gaku*-say so? I suppose the Doll asked the Ma— Mr. Hatter to bring you."

"Well, I *am* staying at the House of *Moji*."

The uniformed person turned around and called in a loud voice, "*Toshi*-san! *Kengaku!*"

And *Toshi* came hopping up on her one leg, which seemed to work like a pogo stick.

"Ah. Arisu *desu, ne*? I think we've met before," said *Toshi*.

Arisu bowed.

"All right. Let's start the *kengaku*. Walk this way please."

Arisu wondered if "walk this way" meant "hop on one leg", but she decided it probably just meant to follow *Toshi*.

They arrived at a place where hundreds and hundreds of small kanji were pouring off a conveyor belt. They all looked like this:

"These are *fun*."

"They do look fun," agreed Arisu.

"Not fun, *fun*. They are minutes. All our other time-products are built from minutes, you know."

"And minutes are pronounced *fun*?"

"Every minute should be fun, and here, they are."

"The kanji shows a *sword* cutting something in half. Because a minute is the smallest *division* of time. For practical purposes anyway.

THE TIME MACHINE

"It is an important kanji that is used in many ways. On its own it is a minute, but it is also used in words like

wakaru, understand (or more accurately, be clear). Because understanding a thing means separating or distinguishing it from other things."

"Can you break that down for me?"

"Exactly. We break something down to understand it. In the case of a *roo*, for example, we *whack* it to break it down. So that is where the word *wak-a-roo* comes from."

Arisu folded her arms. "I don't even like to whack-a-mole, and roos are *much* cuter."

"No roos were whacked in the making of this mnemonic," said *Toshi*. "I'd like to make that clear. However, back to *fun*. Of course, it is the time-meaning that matters here. So, can you tell me what

go-fun means?"

"Five minutes," said Arisu confidently.

"Excellent. Quick learner. Now, if you put 60 *fun* together, you get one of these." *Toshi* skillfully assembled sixty giggling *fun* and they turned into a shiny

ALICE IN KANJI LAND

"This is *ji*, an hour."

"I thought it was ticky-tocky—time."

"Just *toki*, and it is. *Ji* is the glue-name and it means hour. And if we put *ji* together with a number, we get *the* time."

"*The* time?"

"Yes, as in: What's *the* time?"

Toshi picked up an *ichi* and screwed it carefully into a socket on the left-hand side of the *ji* she was holding.

"*Ichi-ji* means one o'clock."

"And if I want to say 'I'll be an hour', I say 'I'll be a *ji*'?"

"No. An hour of time, the space of an hour, is made like this." *Toshi* unscrewed the *ichi* and glued another kanji onto the right of the *ji*.

"Oh! Ji-aida!"

"Not quite. We use the glue-name of *aida*. So it is said *ji-kan*. Notice that there is no kana in this word, unlike the *i* in *nagai aida*. So we are much more likely to be using the glue-name."

"So *aida*'s glue-name is *kan*?"

"Yes. Think of *jikan* as an hour-sized *can* of time. *Wakaru*?"

"*Wakaru*."

"*San-ji* is three o'clock. The hour named 3. *San-jikan* is three hours. Three hour-sized cans of time." *Toshi* skillfully assembled three kanji.

THE TIME MACHINE

"Or one jumbo three-hour can?" asked Arisu.

"It is actually cheaper to buy them that way," said *Toshi*. "Now, you already know the kanji for day and month, and of course—" *Toshi* coughed modestly, "— year."

"Day and month?"

"Exactly the same as sun and moon. But when *o-Hi-sama* is a day, *Hi* is sometimes pronounced *Nichi*."

"Because a day is a *niche* of time?"

"Yes. It is the same pronunciation in *Nihon*, except that the *chi* part gets swallowed in *Nihon*."

"When o-*Tsuki*-sama is a particular month, she is pronounced *gatsu*."

"A *particular* month?"

"Oh yes. The Japanese month names are ridiculously easy to learn. For example, January is

ichi-gatsu. February is *ni-gatsu* and so on. The only thing you have to remember is that *tsuki* becomes *gatsu* in month names."

"Because the months are the twelve *gates* of the year?"

"Quite so."

"So you see, all the time-products made in this factory are assembled from a few simple units. That's why we are so efficient."

"And nothing goes to waste," said Arisu.

"Exactly. So now we need a week. And that is *shuu*."

"I heard of a girl so rich she had a pair of shoes for every week of the year," said Arisu.

"We say *shuu* for every week of the year too," said *Toshi*. "And just as before, if we want to say 'period of a week' we say *shuu-kan*. *San-shuukan* is three weeks. Three week-sized cans of time."

"The kanji has some new bits," said Arisu.

"Yes, it does. Let's break them down so that it becomes more *wakaru*, shall we?"

"You mean so we can *wakaru* it?"

"No, that's English. In Japanese it is normally the *understood-thing* that *wakarus*, not the person understanding it. That confuses a lot of new learners because the textbooks tell them that *wakaru* means understand, which isn't really true. It means become clear.

"So. The main part of this kanji is

This means a round or circuit, and it is enclosed by the Free Radical

which is often called the Upside-Down Box and often gives a sense of rounding or enclosure to what it contains. Inside the box, as you see, we have *tsuchi*, earth, and *kuchi*, mouth. As you know, rounds become square in kanji, so *kuchi* can mean a round thing. She is a great actress, as you may have heard, and plays a lot of roles. With Earth as her prop she plays *roundness*. What is rounder than the Earth?

"So this whole boxful gives us circumference, a round. We find it in

shuu-nen—a full year or anniversary. One year-round.

"You notice that the glue-name of this kanji is *shuu*. And she gives that to the word for week as her regular name.

"To complete the word for week, we need one more Free Radical:

This is a radical that wraps kanji around their left and bottom edges. And it puts them whizzing down the road. Some people call it the water-slide radical, but it is better just to think of it as the *Road of Travel*.

"When we put the circuit kanji on the Road of Travel it becomes

shuu, week. The weeks go around and around, traveling into the future, building into months and years.

"Now here is a very useful kanji that you will use in all kinds of places:

It means *half*. It is a picture of a karate chop breaking three boards in *half*. The first one is already halved and the other two are just about to be as the vertical stroke moves through them. It is called *han* because that is what is doing the halving. A *hand*.

"Why are we learning it here? Because it is very useful for time-talk. For example, what is this?"

"*Han-jikan*, half an hour!" said Arisu.

"Just so. We can also say *han-nen*, half a year. But be careful, because

半分

han-bun does not mean half a minute. It just means *half*. Literally a half-division of something. I take it you know why it is *hanbun* and not han-fun."

"I guess it's a kind of ten-ten hooking," said Arisu.

"That's right. And that covers most of Absolute Time. Now we move on to the Relative Time Department."

15

Relativity

Arisu was shown into another room where she was greeted by a man with bright eyes, wild white hair, and a test tube in his hand.

"Welcome to my laboratory," he said.

Arisu bowed. "Arisu *desu. Yoroshiku onegaishimasu.*"

"Arisu, Arisu. I seem to recall the name. No matter. My name is Isseki. *Yoroshiku, yoroshiku.*

"Time. That's what you've come about, Miss Harris?"

"Arisu. Yes, time."

"It's relative, you know. Time is relative. For example, if we take

ima, now. Well, everything is relative to *now*, isn't it? Past means before *now*. Future means after *now*. *Wakaru?*

"So why does this mean *now*? We have a *Human Roof* and under it what? A Japanese one and an English seven. What does that add up to? 8. What do we get when we lay 8 on its side? Infinity. So you see."

"I am not certain I do see," said Arisu.

"*Now* is infinite. Why? Because *now* is all possible times. Every time is *now* if someone happens to be in it.

"That someone, of course, is the Human Roof. You see, we build our little human existence in what we call 'now'. There is no other time but *now* for us. But *now* keeps changing. Now do you see, Miss Harris?"

"I think so."

"Good. Now, *now* is called *ima*. Why *ima*? Because *I'm a*lways there. I'm never anywhere else in time but now. We can also call it

I'm A

Point *A* at which *I* always *am*.

"Now we can make further calculations based on this. For example:

We add *ima* to *hi* and we get *kyou*, which means *today*.

"We add *ima* to *toshi* and we get *kotoshi*, which means *this year*.

"We add *ima* to *shuu* and we get *konshuu*, which means *this week*."

"I see," said Arisu.

"But notice that it is all purely relative. For example:

RELATIVITY

We add *sen* to *shuu* and we get *senshuu*, last week."

"That's the *sen* of *sensei* and *senpai*," said Arisu.

"Yes, people who went *before* us. But you notice that this week's last week is last week's this week. It is all quite relative. We can also add *sen* to *tsuki* and get last month, which is said *sengetsu*.

"Or we can add *kuru* to any of them

and we get *rai-shuu*, *rai-nen*, etc., meaning *next* week, *next* year, and so on."

"I thought *kuru* meant *come*," said Arisu.

"Of course it does. The *coming* week. The *coming* year. Its glue-name is *rai*. You may have heard the old song '*Comin*' Through the *Rye*'. If not, look it up, because it will help you remember.

"All these calculations are relative to *ima*. But we can just as easily take some other point in time, such as

which means *noon*. I always associate this with 1000—I don't know if you've met *Sen*-san. I usually get on very well with numbers. However, *Sen*-san is—well, enough of that. This is *Sen*-san who has finally put his hat on straight for once. And then put *another hat* on top of that at such a crazy angle it is practically falling off. I've really seen him do that, you know. Anyway, this means *noon*. Because *Sen*-san always gets up at noon. Can you believe that?

"Ahem. In any case, noon is pronounced *go* because that is when we *go* for lunch (not to be confused with *go* meaning *five*, which is when we *go* for tea).

"So taking noon as our starting-point we can have

go-zen, which means before noon, or *morning*…"

"That *zen* is *mae*, meaning front, isn't it?" said Arisu.

"Yes. *Zen* is the glue-name."

"Is it coincidence that it sounds like *sen*, which means something similar?"

"No, it isn't. Sounds have definite tendencies in Japanese. They aren't very calculable though. To continue, we can also have

go-go. Afternoon."

"I haven't seen that second kanji before," said Arisu.

"That's the partner of *mae*. *Mae* is front and this is rear or behind. On its own it is pronounced *ushiro* because…"

Professor Isseki started laughing in the most childish manner.

"Because what?" asked Arisu.

Professor Isseki tried to tell her but was choked with convulsive laughter.

Arisu waited patiently.

Finally the professor calmed down enough to get it out.

RELATIVITY

"I am sorry, Miss Harris. This is really so very funny. I always think *ushiro* means behind because I think of a monkey with a *white* (*shiro*) *U-shaped behind*!"

The professor just managed to stutter that out and then became a lost cause, cachinnating helplessly for a good five minutes. Arisu thought it was most un-professorly behavior, especially after his starchy disapproval of *Sen*-san.

"Forgive me, Miss Harris," said the professor, wiping his eyes with a large handkerchief. "Let us take a closer look at this kanji."

"You mean *ushi*…"

"Please don't say that word, Miss Harris. I shan't be able to continue if you do."

"I am sorry, Professor."

"My fault entirely. Just a little weakness of mine. Very well. It isn't surprising if you don't understand the second kanji in *go-go*. It contains three Free Radicals, none of which you have met yet. Now pay attention, because all three are very important.

"As a matter of fact, you have half-met the first one. Quite literally. It is the top half of *ito*, thread or string.

It gets called 'short thread', though whether that is because it represents a short thread or because it is a short form of the thread kanji, I don't know. I tend to think of the long one as thread and the short one as string.

"The Free Radical on the right is

As you can see this is related to

the *hito* side-radical. While the regular *hito* side-radical represents a person standing still, the one with the extra line on top represents a *person going* or *walking*. We call it the *go-hito*."

"The extra line is a whoosh-line," suggested Arisu.

"I shouldn't wonder," said the professor, who didn't look as if he knew what a whoosh-line was.

"Now the last of the three is

This one means winter. Probably because it is the hand Free Radical seen in *tomo(dachi)*

with a katakana NO before it. In very cold climates like Hokkaido, winter was called 'no hands season' because everyone wore gloves and you never saw any hands.

"So we have *go-hito* plus *string* plus *winter*. Now we can of course parody the famous poetic line:

'If winter comes, can spring be far behind?'
with
'If *winter goes*, can *string* be far *behind*?'

"Or we can see it as Jack Frost—a *person traveling* through late autumn, dragging *winter* on a *string behind* him. Either way,

means *behind*, and its glue-name is *go*. Let's not even think about its other name.

"In relative time-terms, we can remember *go-zen* and *go-go* by remembering that in the mornings Japanese people *go* to *zen* meditation where they sit quietly, but in the afternoons they get up and *go-go*!"

Professor Isseki started giggling.

"Are you all right, Professor?" asked Arisu.

"Oh yes. I just thought of that word."

"*Ushiro*, you mean—behind?"

"Oh! You *said* it!" The professor collapsed into helpless paroxysms of laughter.

There was a respectful knock on the door and *Toshi* came in without waiting for an answer. She looked at the professor, who was screaming with laughter, and then turned to Arisu.

"This happens occasionally," she said. "Nothing to worry about, but we'd best leave him to it."

Arisu followed *Toshi* as she hopped out of the laboratory and back into the big room with all the clocks.

"Thank you so much for honoring our humble establishment with your visit," she said.

"No, no, it is for me to thank you," said Arisu. "I have learned so much today."

"Here is a little present to show our appreciation," said *Toshi*. She handed Arisu a small velvet bag tied with pink ribbon.

"There are five freshly made minutes in here. Please use them wisely. And do be careful with them—they are sharp."

"Thank you so much," said Arisu. She stood a little uncertain what to do next.

"Well, I suppose it'll be getting on for lunch time," said *Toshi* hintingly.

"Oh yes! I'm supposed to go back to the House of *Moji* for lunch," said Arisu. "But I'm not sure I know the way back. It was such a winding way and Mr. Hatter walks so fast and keeps taking wrong turnings and going back on himself."

"Hmm. If you check your Kanjidex, you might find you have enough points to get The Compass," said *Toshi*.

Arisu opened her Kanjidex. There were lots of pictures of the kanji she had learned. Not much else as far as she could see.

"Try saying 'Compass'," said *Toshi*.

"Co—compass!" said Arisu in a loud voice.

Pfoom!

She found herself in what looked like the inside of a cave with nothing in it but a red treasure chest with bright gold trimmings.

She moved toward the treasure chest, but an invisible barrier seemed to prevent her from reaching it.

A feminine robotic voice shouted:

"*Tarinai! Tarinai!* Incomplete pairs!"

16

Inside the Treasure Cave

"*Tarinai! Tarinai!* Incomplete pairs!" repeated the robotic voice. Arisu realized it was coming from her Kanjidex.

"What does that mean?" asked Arisu.

"Incomplete pair 1: *kuru* without *iku*," said the Kanjidex. "Recommended action: Locate *kuru*."

Arisu flipped through screens on the Kanjidex until she came to

"*Kuru*, come," said the Kanjidex. "Antonymic pair: *iku*."

"Meaning *go*?" asked Arisu.
The Kanjidex made a bleepy, bell-like sound.
Pin-pon! Pin-pon! Pin-pon!
Arisu realized she had guessed correctly.
"That's the *go-hito* Free Radical on the left," said Arisu.
Pin-pon!
"And there's little *Ichi* at the top right."
Pin-pon!
"I'm not sure what that thing is under her. Is that a Free Radical?"

"That figure is not an official Free Radical," said the robotic voice. "However, it appears frequently and has been designated the Bus Stop by the Kanji Land Explorers' Society."

"I see. So the *go-hito* goes by bus."

"In this kanji *go-hito* is usually conceived as walking. Passes one bus stop after another. Do you remember the name?"

"*Iku.*"

"Correct. *Iku* added to Kanjidex. Pair *iku / kuru* now complete."

"Can I open the treasure chest now?"

"Non-advised. Incomplete pairs remain *kara.*"

"What are they?"

"Incomplete pair 2: *miru* without *kiku.*"

Arisu flipped through Kanjidex screens to

"*Miru*, see," said the Kanjidex. "Natural pair: *kiku*, hear.

"Why, that's a *mimi*. An ear."

"Correct so far."

"Standing inside the *Great Sun Gates.*"

Pin-pon!

"*Sun gates* allow perception into human mind. This perception is audial—enters via human *ear* apparatus. English term: *hear*. Japanese term: *kiku.*"

"I can imagine *Sen*-san saying, 'Well, ain't that a *kick* in the *ear*'."

"Personal mnemonic registered. Does *kiku* now *wakaru* for user Arisu-sama?"

"*Wakaru*," said Arisu.

"*Kiku* added. Pair *miru / kiku* now complete."

"Then I can open the treasure chest?"

"Non-advised. Incomplete pairs remain. Incomplete pair 3: *naka* without *soto*."

Arisu looked up

"*Naka*, inside. Antonymic pair: *soto*, outside," said the Kanjidex.

"That's *evening* on the left," said Arisu.

Pin-pon!

"I'm not sure about the other one though."

"Free Radical subdex indicates new Free Radical. Initiating Free Radical:

This Free Radical is *Magic Wand*."

"It looks like the bottom of *shita*."

"Ancient magicians hung wands from ceiling when not in use. Some sources say this is origin of *shita*."

"So *soto* is *evening* plus *Magic Wand* and means *outside*?"

"Correct. Magicians do outdoor magic in the evening. In former times witchcraft was illegal and could only be done *outside* the house after dark."

"And quietly. *Soto voce*, you might say," said Arisu.

"Discretion was advised at that period."

"And afterwards they said 'and *so to* bed' and returned inside."

"That probability exists. *Soto* may be used to make various words. Example:

"Outside-person?" said Arisu.

"Affirmative. It is pronounced *gai-jin*. *Gai* is on-reading of *soto*. *Jin* is on-reading of *hito*. Meaning: foreigner, non-Japanese person."

"Is on-reading the same as glue-name?"

"Correct. Does *soto* now *wakaru* for user Arisu-sama?"

"*Wakaru.*"

"*Soto* added to Kanjidex. User Arisu-sama may now proceed to treasure chest."

Arisu walked over to the treasure chest and opened it. Inside was a round object, which she carefully lifted out.

Da-da-da-DA!

A triumphant four-note chime sounded and the Kanjidex announced:

"You found The Compass!"

Arisu looked at The Compass. "How do you use it?" she asked.

"First it is necessary to read the kanji. The one at the top is

kita. This means *north*."

"It has the *spoon* on the right," said Arisu.

"Correct," said the Kanjidex. "However, many members of the Kanji Land Explorers' Society prefer to see this as two people back to back."

"Why?" asked Arisu.

"Because the North is cold. When it is cold, Japanese children play a game of standing back to back and pushing their backs against each other to keep warm."

"Really?" said Arisu.

"This is factual information," said the Kanjidex.

"And since north is the highest, *kita* flies above the others like a kite."

"Recorded. Directly below *kita* is *minami*."

"That must mean *south* then."

Pin-pon!

"It looks as if *Sen*-san is in that box with his hat straight again."

"*Sen*-san with hat straight is *dry*," said the Kanjidex.

"Why?" asked Arisu.

"This is rumor so please do not repeat to others," said the Kanjidex.

"I promise," said Arisu.

"Rumor is that *Sen*-san drinks too much. When *Sen*-san does not drink, *Sen*-san is able to put hat on straight. Thus *Sen-san with straight hat is dry*."

"It also looks like a washing-line pole for drying washing."

"The *South* is hot and therefore dry," continued the Kanjidex. "However, it is *supposed* to be dry, so don't worry. Notice that the dry element is crowned with the two 'horns' of the Crown of Rightness and the whole thing is properly boxed in the Upside-Down Box. So the *South* is a *self-contained* place where *dryness* is *proper*."

"And there is a cross above it."

"Naturally that is the *Southern Cross*, which can be seen *above* places *south* of the equator."

"And south is the lowest, so you could say it's the *minimum* or *minami*."

"On the right of The Compass is

higashi, east."

"This one is easy," said Arisu. "The sun rising in the morning, still low enough to be seen through the branches of a tree."

"Affirmative. And it is called *higashi* because…"

"Because *Hi*, the sun, *gashes* the still-dark sky with streaks of wonderful light."

"Recorded. And on the left is

nishi, west."

"It looks like a four, doesn't it? Perhaps because we say north, south, east, west, so west is the *fourth* of the *four*.

"Only, the top of the box is doubled and the legs have popped out a bit. That part at the top where the box-lid is doubled looks like a two. So naturally it is pronounced *ni-shi*—two-four."

"Recorded. Compass directions complete."

"What now?"

"*What—nani*."

"I didn't mean... Oh well..."

"It is regular *side-hito* at the left, and the *Bus Stop*, and little *Kuchi*."

"*Bus Stop* and *Kuchi* together make *can*."

"Like a can of peas?"

"Negative. Like 'can do', able. This kanji is the *ka* in *kawaii*, which means can love, lovable."

"If you have a mouth at a Bus Stop you *can* call a taxi. Or you *can* sing songs to the people waiting and try to make money. Or you *can* eat a sandwich while you wait. In fact, you *can* do a lot of things at a Bus Stop, provided you have a mouth."

"That is correct."

"So this

is *person can*."

"Positive."

"Person can *what*?"

Pin-pon! Pin-pon! Pin-pon!

"That was the answer?"

"Yes. When someone says 'person can', response is always 'person can *what*?' Therefore the *person-can* kanji means *what*."

"And it is said *nani*?"

"Correct. It is named after the famous British nursemaid, *Nanny Watt*. A friend of Miss Mary Poppins. It can also be abbreviated to *nan*. The kanji pronunciation. Not Miss Watt. Miss Watt is averse to abbreviations. Does this *wakaru*?"

"I think so. The kanji is pronounced *nani* and means the question-word *what*. It is sometimes abbreviated to *nan*."

"Correct. Recorded."

"But what I meant by 'What now?' was 'What do I do now?' This cave seems to have no exits."

"Correct. Cave is a one-screen Player Reward Location. Normal movement options are not present."

"So—um—how do I leave?"

INSIDE THE TREASURE CAVE

"Compass directions have changed values in direction-less locations. *Kita* to go forward, *minami* to go back."

"I suppose I want to go forward—" thought Arisu. She touched the *kita* kanji on The Compass and the cave faded out.

17

The Road to Nowhere

As the cave faded out, Arisu found herself in a little street with shops along one side.

"Where is this?" Arisu asked the Kanjidex. But there was no reply.

"How do I get back to the House of *Moji* from here?" she shouted into the Kanjidex. Still no reply.

"*Ojou-chan*. Kindly stop shouting in the street. It isn't seemly." Arisu turned around and saw the White Rabbit.

"Meiji-san," said Arisu, remembering the White Rabbit's name. "*Gomen nasai.* I was talking to my Kanjidex."

"Well, you know what *that's* the first sign of," said the White Rabbit.

"Honestly, it talked to me before."

"In a regular location?"

"No, it was a Player Reward Area."

"Well, there you are."

"Where am I?"

"On the road.

Michi, road. You understand?"

"Not quite. But that's the Road of Travel, isn't it? Along the side and bottom. And an eye and the Horns of Rightness, or whatever they're called. And *Ichi* too who often goes with them."

"Hmf. Fine mess you're making of that. It's not *wakaru*-ing properly at all, now is it?"

THE ROAD TO NOWHERE

"I suppose not."
"Start with the eye and the drop on top of it."

"It's like *Shiro*, only with *Me* instead of *Hi*."
"You could say that. A lot of people think of that drop as a nose. The sticking-out thing that lives near your eyes. Japanese people point at their noses when they mean themselves, the way *gaijin* point at their chests. You see this kanji in

jibun, oneself."
"Isn't that a minute?"
"A minute is a division of time. *Jibun* is that division of humanity that is oneself. You have heard people say 'for my part, I think...'"
"Yes—"
"Well, that's what *jibun* means. My part. The *part* of things that is *me*.
"Now if we put the Crown of Rightness on *ji*,

it becomes *kubi*, neck. The name comes from Squarehead Land, apparently. People with square heads have *cubi*cal necks."

"Why is *neck* the Crown of Rightness on self?"

"The Crown of Rightness can indicate completeness or something that sums up the whole."

"My *neck* sums up my *self*?"

"As a body part, *kubi* is definitely *neck*. However, it is used in many expressions as if it meant head. We say a neck-less person, not a headless person. And the *kubi* radical is used in expressions meaning chief or primary where English would say *head*."

"I see—"

"What do you see?"

"I mean *wakaru*."

"Good. So put the head-ness of *kubi* together with the Road of Travel

and you have the *Way*. The Great Road. The on-reading of this kanji is *Dou*. That is the same as Chinese *Tao*. It doesn't just mean a literal road. It also means the Way. For example, *Juu-dou* (judo) is the Way of Gentleness. *Ken-dou* (kendo) is the Way of the Sword. A *Dou-jou* (dojo) is a Place of the Way.

"I wonder if there is an example using kanji you might know. Yes, I think so..."

"*Sky-hand way?*" asked Arisu.

"In a way. The *sky* radical isn't said *sora* here. It is said *kara*, meaning empty. The sky is the biggest empty space on earth, after all."

"*Kara*—"

"Yes. As in *kara-oke*. *Oke* here is short for English orchestra. *Empty orchestra* means orchestration with no vocal. So people can sing it for themselves."

"So that word means *empty-hand way*?"

"Exactly. *Kara-te* is empty hand. Hand with no weapon."

"*Kara-te*. Oh, karate."

"Please don't pronounce it in that barbaric manner. It is *kara-te*. And *Kara-te-dou* is the *Way of Kara-te*."

"Of course, the kanji can also mean a literal road. *Michi*."

"Because of all the Michelin tires that go along it?"

"Very possibly." Meiji pulled out his pocket watch. "But I must be going along too."

"Oh, one moment please. I need to get to the House of *Moji*. How do I get there?"

"On this road? This road is a Shopping Street, not a Traveling Street. You can't get anywhere on this road."

"Not even to another road?"

"Not even."

"So how do I leave?"

"I'm not sure you do."

"But you said *you* were going along."

"I am I and you are you. *I* get all over the place as you may have noticed. I even get to Human Land. *Your* powers of locomotion, on the other hand, appear to be strictly limited."

"*I* get all over the place too, as *you* may have noticed," said Arisu heatedly.

The White Rabbit muttered something that sounded like *nama-iki-na*. Aloud he said, "Then you won't need my help, will you? And I must be on my way. Thanks to you I am very, very late." The White Rabbit started to leave.

"*Gomen nasai*," said Arisu, bowing deeply. She was conscious that she really had been very rude.

"Try asking at an…"

shouted the White Rabbit over his shoulder. And with that he was gone.

"Now what's the use of that when I don't know what the kanji is?" said Arisu to herself.

She put on her best smile and said to a passing hedgehog, "*Ano, sumimasen*. Can you tell me what this kanji—"

"Very sorry. Terrible hurry," said the hedgehog and walked by.

"Oh dear. Everyone seems to be in a hurry," said Arisu.

She tried a field mouse.

"*Ano, sumimasen*. This kanji—"

"So sorry. Don't have a minute to spare," said the field mouse.

Arisu remembered the present she had received at the Time Machine. She reached into the bag and took out a

She offered it to the field mouse.

"Why, thank you. Are you sure it's all right to take this?"

"You are most welcome," said Arisu. "But I was wondering if you could tell me about this kanji…"

"Oh yes. You'll find a lot of those in this street."
"It's a *Magic Wand*, isn't it? With *Kuchi*."
"That it is. And in a *cave* too."
"A *cave*?"
"Yes. It's a Free Radical.

It gets called a dotted cliff sometimes. But it's easier to think of it as a cave."
"What is in the cave?"
"*Uranai*."
"Am I?" said Arisu, wondering what a *nai* was.
"*Uranai* means fortune-telling.

Take a mouth and a magic wand and you get fortune-telling."
"With planets like *Uranus*, I suppose."
"That's one method. Anyways, back in the old, old days, old ladies set up in caves telling people's fortunes for a living. Everyone came to them and after a while they realized they could make more money if they kept some eggs and potatoes to sell to the people when they came to have their hands read. And that's how the first shops started. We call them

o-mise. Or just *mise* if you don't want to make the word pretty. Probably because they sell *miso* soup.

"The glue-name is *ten*. Because you have to have at least ten things in store before you can call yourself a shop. Once you know that, you can make words like

"Hmm," said Arisu. "No kana, so glue-names all around is a good bet. So is that *rai-ten*?"

"That's right, *raiten*. And it means just what you'd think. *Coming to the shop*."

"There's a *word* for *coming to the shop*?" asked Arisu in surprise.

"Yes," said the field mouse. "Glue-names are interesting like that. You can glue together all kinds of kanji to make 'words' that would be thought of as 'phrases' in English. Once you get used to a lot of kanji and their glue-names, you don't necessarily need to know the 'word' in advance so long as you know the 'words' inside the 'word'. Of course, whether the whole idea 'word' is the same in Japanese and English is—too much for my little mousey mind. You'd have to ask someone like Professor Isseki.

"Oh dear. Chattering on and now that minute's all used up. Don't they just fly? I must fly too!"

But the field mouse didn't fly at all. She just scurried away.

"So the White Rabbit meant that I should ask in a shop," said Arisu.

She walked into the nearest shop. It had all kinds of goods piled up all over the store in a higgledy-piggledy jumble.

THE ROAD TO NOWHERE

"*Irasshaimase*," shouted someone from behind the counter. It seemed to be a pig.

"Arisu *desu*."

"I'm Higgledy Pig," said the storekeeper. "Arisu? Why, don't I remember an Arisu from when I was a baby? No, probably not."

"Do you have a minute?" asked Arisu.

"Boxes of them," said Higgledy Pig. "I just got a fresh consignment from the Time Machine."

"Is this an *o-mise*?" asked Arisu.

"It's certainly not a *dou-jou*," said Higgledy Pig. "Yes, this is a *mise*. A shop. A place where lots of things are put to be sold. If you happen to know any French, *mise* is the French word for put."

"Not *o-mise*?" asked Arisu.

"*Mise*, *o-mise*, either is all right for you. Depends how pretty you want to make it. Not all right for me though. I can't call *this* shop *o-mise* because it's my shop. Not very polite to glorify one's own things. So I just call it *mise*, and what I do is

uru."

"*Uru*? Like Thor's hammer?"

"Well, I'd *sell* that if Thor was in the market. *Uru* means *sell*."

"Ah. That is human legs, the wa-shaped crown, and *tsuchi*, earth," said Arisu, feeling rather pleased with herself.

"Not so fast," said Higgledy Pig. "Take another look at '*tsuchi*'."

Arisu looked carefully.

"The top horizontal is longer than the base," said Arisu. "Does that make a difference?"

"A *big* difference," said Higgledy Pig. "It is quite another kanji.

is *samurai*."

"Really?"

"Really. In the old days the *samurai* stretched out their arms over all the earth."

"Even outside Japan?"

"Outside Japan doesn't count. Anyway, when the Great Samurai Days were over they had to get off their horses and walk around on their own *Human Legs*. Instead of serving the Crown they would set up a *crown* on a spare *pair of legs* and use it as a table to *sell* things.

"It was the only way they could survive."

"How sad."

"Not too sad. Many of the great Japanese companies that are known all over the world were started by those samurai.

"So, have you come to…"

THE ROAD TO NOWHERE

"To what?"

"To buy. This is *kau*, buy."

"That's the seashell, *Kai*!" said Arisu excitedly.

"It is," said Higgledy Pig. "And she kind-of lends her pronunciation to the word. The stem of *kau* is also *kai*, as in *kaimono*—buy-thing, which means *shopping*. We call *Kai* the *Happy Clam*. And as you may know, *Happy Clam* often indicates *money* when she appears in other kanji. *Seashells* were once used as money, and even today '*clams*' can be slang for money."

"And people talk about 'shelling out' money," put in Arisu.

"That's right, they do."

"But what is the other part?"

"That's a Free Radical."

It's called the *Net*. The kanji is obvious enough. When you go out with *money* to *net* the things you need, that's called *kau*, buy. If you happen to know any German, the German word for buy is *kauf*.

"So, what did you want to *kau*?"

"Nothing, I'm afraid. I wanted to ask something."

"What was that?"

"Since this is a Shopping Street and not a Traveling Street, I wanted to know how to get out of it."

"What's wrong with this street?"

"Nothing. Nothing at all," said Arisu hastily. "It's just that I've got to get back to the House of *Moji* for lunch."

"The House of *Moji*, *ne*—That's a bit beyond me. Why not try the shop next door? Baron Cheshire runs it. Very learned individual. I'm sure he can help you."

"Thank you so much," said Arisu.

"No, thank *you*," said Higgledy Pig.

161

18

No-Tea with the Baron

Arisu left Higgledy Pig's *mise* and entered the *mise* next door. It was full of shelves containing what must have been at least ten thousand books.

Arisu looked at the spines of the books in fascination. She could read the hiragana, of course. And now she could even recognize a few of the kanji.

Arisu spent quite a long time looking at them, thinking rapturously of how much wisdom and how many adventures must lie in them and how she would one day be able to read them all.

Lost in thought, she was startled by a voice from behind her, although it was a very calm, well-modulated voice.

"*Irasshaimase*. Welcome to my humble *mise*."

Arisu turned around to see a cat wearing a grey tuxedo and grey silk hat. The bow tie was blue and the waistcoat under the tuxedo a dark red. All the colors seemed exquisitely well chosen and toned together to perfection. Most notable of all was the cat's remarkable smile.

"B–Baron Cheshire?" stammered Arisu.

"At your service," said the Baron.

Arisu bowed deeply. "*Yo—yoroshiku onegaishimasu. Arisu desu.*"

"*Kochira koso*," said the Baron, sweeping off his hat in a perfect bow. "I see you are interested in books, Arisu-chan."

"I have always had an *affinity* with books," said Arisu, using one of her fanciest words for the Baron's benefit. "Sometimes I feel that I *am* a character in a book."

"I understand the feeling," said the Baron. "I have it too, though in my case I am never entirely sure whether it is a book or a motion picture. I hope it is a book, because books are pure words, aren't they, and words are the foundation of everything."

"They certainly seem to be in Kanji Land."

"Everywhere, I believe. Grammar is nothing but the structure of the universe reflected in words. Pure grammar, I mean. Not this or that language but the underlying Archetype of Word."

"I—"

"Forgive me. Just some nonsensical notion of mine. But look. Isn't this beautiful?

"It means *say*. It is simply *i*, though the usual word is pronounced *iu*. I always feel one is getting close to the roots of things in words that only have mother-sounds."

"Mother-sounds?"

"Vowels. A, I, U, E and O. The other sounds are all child-sounds because they all belong to one of the Mothers. Except for that curious motherless child that everyone loves so much:

"But I am getting carried away, aren't I? I love them all so dearly. We were talking about *iu*, weren't we?"

"About me?" asked Arisu.

"No, about *iu*. Though it is pronounced rather like *you*, isn't it? Don't you think she is perfect? Just little *Kuchi* with four lines of sound radiating from her, growing and then fading. Just like real sound. That is pure speech, I think. The *sound* of the Primordial *Mouth*. The very essence of speech, before all complications."

Arisu felt a little thrill. Although his words were complicated and confusing, she did catch the drift of his thoughts and found them somehow exhilarating.

"Anyway, you don't need all my blather for your Kanjidex. Just

Means *say*. Pronounced *iu*. Like *you*. *You say*. After that, speech enters into the Round of Being and it all becomes more complicated. But no less beautiful, I think.

"When living beings speak they need to have a *tongue*."

"That is *Kuchi* and *Sen*-san," said Arisu.

"Yes. A *tongue* is what allows our *mouth* to speak a *thousand* different things. It is pronounced *shita*."

"The same as *down*," said Arisu.

"Indeed. You have heard the expression 'down in the mouth'. The tongue is what is always *down* in the mouth."

"*Kuchi no naka no shita*," said Arisu.

"Now, if we put *i(u)* and *shita* together, we get words put into practice. Actually said by the tongue.

"*Hanasu*. Speak or talk."

"*Hanna* and *Sue* never stop talking!" said Arisu.

"And if we want to say *language*, we use this kanji…"

"*Say* with *five mouths*?" said Arisu.

"Yes. We have *i(u)*, *kuchi* and *go*. Five here means *many*. A language is something *said* by *many mouths*. You probably already know words that use this kanji, such as

Nihon-go (Japanese). Also *Ei-go* (English) and *Furansu-go* (French). Notice that *go* meaning five takes her pronunciation with her into this kanji. She is a Sound Sister."

"A Sound Sister?"

"Yes. A Sound Sister is a kanji element that usually carries her pronunciation with her into any kanji she takes part in. Mostly this affects the glue-names of those other kanji. So the Sound Sisters are most active in words that are made up entirely of kanji. Quite a lot of elements do this to some extent. You may have noticed a few already. But the Sound Sisters do it much more often."

"Are there a lot of Sound Sisters?"

"Around a hundred really active ones, influencing thousands of words. You don't need to worry about them too much yet, but they will help you a lot as you progress.

"But we were really talking about books, weren't we? Forgive me for getting carried away with my pet subject, language."

"Oh no, Baron, it was fascinating."

"Thank you so much for humoring me. Now if we want books we need to do this:

Read."

"Why, isn't that *i(u)* with *uru*, sell?"

"Exactly so. Until not so long ago, the only way you could *sell speech* was if you put it into *readable* form—a book or a magazine or suchlike."

"How is it said?"

"*Yomu*. Apparently this was originally bookworm slang. Bookworms, as you know, eat books as they read them. Some books are tastier than others, so when they have read a book they give it a grade on the Yum-O-Meter. Any book that had been read by a bookworm had also been Y-O-Med, so *yomu* came to mean *read*.

"However, before anyone can read, someone needs to

NO-TEA WITH THE BARON

kaku, write."

"There is *o-Hi-sama*," said Arisu. "I am not sure about the rest."

"The rest is a Free Radical," said the Baron. "This is the *writing-brush* radical:

As you know, traditional Japanese writing is done with a brush, not a pen. This radical shows a three-fingered hand holding a long brush. At the bottom we see the bristles splaying out sideways. Of course, writing-brush bristles don't really splay out sideways, but this is a stylized way of representing them."

"So writing is a *writing brush* with the *sun* underneath it?"

"Yes. Writing was considered so special that what the brush writes is like a shining sun. Quite literally enlightening, one might say."

"The writing brush loses its bottom in the *kaku* kanji," said Arisu.

"Yes, that happens fairly often. When elements are combined they often get a little shortened."

"And is it true that the pronunciation *kaku* is because writing was first perfected by witches who *cackle* while they write their spells?"

"That rumor is quite unfounded. As is the more plausible but equally false rumor that the first writing was done with frosting on a *cake*. Speaking of which, would you care for a cup of tea?"

Suddenly Arisu remembered why she had come into the Baron's *o-mise* in the first place.

"Oh, Baron. I have been so forgetful. Your wonderful talk about talk and words about words have enchanted me. But I came here for quite another reason."

"If I have amused you for a brief moment, I am honored more than I can say," said the Baron. His wide, enchanting smile became wider than ever. "And if I can serve you in some other way also, that will be my greatest pleasure."

"I—I was supposed to go back to the House of *Moji* for lunch," she said.

"Hmm. It isn't quite lunch time yet, but the House of *Moji* is rather far from here."

"I did a foolish thing."

"We all do foolish things occasionally. What was it?"

"I got into a Player Reward Area and pressed the option to go forward. Of course, I should have gone back, to return to the House of *Moji*."

"Well, in case they worry about you maybe we should contact them."

"How can we do that?"

"Have you heard of the telephone?"

"The telephone—?"

"Yes. Wonderful device. It works by this..."

"What's that?" asked Arisu. "It looks like *ame*—rain—on a *field*."

"Yes, that's what it is."

Arisu looked puzzled. She had never heard of a telephone that worked by rain on a field.

"I should perhaps explain further," said the Baron. "Rain on a field means lightning. It is pronounced *kaminari*. Actually, there is an amusing story behind it. A certain gentleman who had had just a little too much to drink—I'm not going to say who it was—was walking across the field when he heard a great peal of thunder. He was so confused that he thought it was his friend Harry knocking on the door, so he shouted *'Come in, 'Arry'* and who should come in but a great flash of lightning landing right next to him and burning a hole in the grass. Ever since then, lightning has been represented by *rain* over a *field* and called *come-in-'Arry*."

"But what has that to do with the telephone?" asked Arisu.

"Ah well, you see, years later people learned how to harness the power of lightning. They ran a *wire* from the *field* to houses or lamp-posts or whatever they wanted to have electricity.

There is the lightning-field with the wire running out of it."

"And that powers the telephone," said Arisu, seeing the point at last.

"Exactly. A telephone is

electric-speak. It is called *den-wa*. *Den* is electricity, you see, and *wa* is the glue-name of *hanasu*, speech. That is because the kanji is *W*ord *A*nd tongue—W.A."

Without more ado, the Baron picked up a large black telephone with gold trimmings and dialed a number on the big round golden dial.

"Hello, is that the House of *Moji*? — No, I don't need one. I have a perfectly good one already. I am wearing it right now. — Yes, of course you made it. I would never buy one from anyone but you. — Please listen for one moment. Arisu-san is here and I believe she should be there. — I see. Might it be possible to speak to someone a little more… — Very well. I am going to put her on the train. Please be at the station to meet her. — Very well then, send the maid to the station. Please don't forget."

The Baron put down the telephone.

"He does make very good hats, but really—"

"I know just what you mean," said Arisu.

"Now, we're going to put you on one of these…"

"Electric car—den-kuruma?"

"This is the glue-name of *kuruma*. That is *sha*. As in *shariot*."

"Isn't that *chariot*?"

"Forgive my slightly French pronunciation. *Den-sha* is a train. *Electric vehicle*."

"How exciting! A Kanji-Land train!"

"Is it exciting?" said the Baron. "I am glad. I am sure you will enjoy it. Let's go to the station."

As they walked briskly along the street Arisu asked, "How would you just say 'electricity'?"

"*Den-ki*," said the Baron.

"Oh. *Electric Spirit*."

"Yes. We often use that to mean 'the lights' in a house. 'Turn off the *denki*'. Back when electricity was new and experimental, it was all controlled by Father from his den. So you needed the *den key* to turn on the lights.

"But here we are."

They were at a big building with a sign on the front that read

"What's that?"

"*Eki*. The station."

Arisu jumped up and down. "Because it's so *Eki*-citing!"

"I am glad it pleases you so much."

"What is the kanji? I can't make head nor tail of it."

"It is a bit confusing, isn't it? The left-hand side is a radical:

It is also a kanji in its own right."

"So not a *Free* Radical," said Arisu.

"Exactly. It means horse."

"It doesn't look much like a horse to me."

"It doesn't, does it? At the bottom you can see four legs and a tail and at the top a big checkered horse-blanket. Maybe."

"Mm. I suppose so."

"Those four squips (to use the technical term) at the bottom usually mean *fire*. But here it might be better to think of them as the horse's four legs."

ALICE IN KANJI LAND

"A fiery horse with the speed of light—" said Arisu.

"Exactly. That's just it. The horse was originally called *Zoomer*. But the baby always said it *Uma*, and that name kind of stuck."

"So *Uma* is a horse?"

"Quite so. But we were talking about stations. They were originally stagecoach stations and had an *Uma-the-Zoomer* sign on the front. Later when they became railway stations they put a big R next to the *Uma-the-Zoomer* to show that they were railway stations, not literal horse stations."

The Baron put Arisu on a train and stood outside the window looking very, very dashing in his tall hat, saying a few final words to her.

"It has been a great pleasure, Arisu-chan. We feel in some way like kindred souls, don't you think? I hope we may *au* again."

"*Au?*" said Arisu.

"Meet," said the Baron. "It is called *au*. Au is the chemical symbol for gold. Because meeting with dear people is golden."

"Words made only with mother-sounds really do come close to the root of things, don't they?" said Arisu.

"They do. The kanji contains a new Free Radical:

It looks just like a katakana MU, doesn't it? And it means myself. Do you remember how a Japanese person points to herself?"

"She points to her nose," said Arisu.

NO-TEA WITH THE BARON

"Well, the *mu* Free Radical is a nose. And therefore it means myself."

"And the rest of the kanji is *Human Roof* and *Ni*, two," said Arisu.

"That's right. Two selves meet under a roof."

"It would be fun if we could meet under a roof again sometime, Baron," said Arisu.

"Yes. We never did have that cup of tea, did we?" said the Baron.

The train whistle blew loudly and the train started to move away. Arisu watched the Baron as he stood smiling on the platform, waving his silk handkerchief. As the train gathered speed, he became smaller and fainter, until nothing could be seen of him but his smile.

19

The Train of Events

When even the Baron's smile was no longer visible, Arisu sat down and looked around the railway carriage. Most of the seats were occupied by playing cards.

Several of the playing cards were not in their seats. They seemed to be building something on the carriage floor. First they put down a box, and then a large upside-down box over it, then another box on top of that and then a top hat on top of everything.

"What is that?" asked Arisu, unable to restrain her curiosity.

"That's *high*," said the Three of Clubs.

"I can see that," said Arisu. "But what *is* it?"

"*High*," said the Two of Hearts. "That's what it is. *High*."

The Four of Spades climbed onto the top of the pile and took down a bag that was hanging from a tack high on the carriage wall.

"It's pronounced *takai* and it means *high*," explained the Four of Hearts.

"The high tack was *takai*," said the Four of Spades, climbing down with the bag, "but we built the kanji even *takai*-er."

A giggling sound came from the kanji itself. It was little *Kuchi*, mouth, the Great Actress.

"Rather a successful role, hi-hi! This time I play *two* boxes!"

The cards gathered around the bag that had been fetched down from the *takai* high tack. The Four of Hearts pulled out a fish bowl.

THE TRAIN OF EVENTS

"There we are, *Sakana*-chan. Now you can look out of the window and enjoy the journey."

Inside the bowl was the strangest fish Arisu had ever seen.

"That's a *fish?*" asked Arisu.

"Of course it's a fish," said the Four of Spades. "What does it look like to you? A monkey?"

"A road roller?" put in the Three of Clubs.

"The Oofle Tower?" squeaked the little Two of Hearts.

"It looks like a field with a clamp on top. And at the bottom is

which is a Free Radical that played the horse's legs in *Uma-the-Zoomer*. But it's really *fire*, isn't it?"

"That's right," said the Four of Hearts, smiling. "So if you can see all that you didn't really need to ask, did you?"

"I can see all *that*," said Arisu. "What I can't see is how all that amounts to a fish."

"She doesn't *amount* at all," said the Four of Spades. "It's the *takai* boxes that *amounted*. Little *Sakana*-chan just swims."

Sakana-chan swam happily around her bowl while the Two of Hearts held it up to the window so that *Sakana*-chan could see the sunny countryside rolling by.

The Four of Hearts tapped Arisu on the shoulder and beckoned her to come to the far side of the carriage.

"The truth," she said in a whisper, "is that we don't want to say this in front of *Sakana*-chan because it will upset her. That clamp on the field means a bad harvest. Very little good food coming from the fields. Consequently very little to cook on the fire during winter. Do you understand?"

"I think so," said Arisu. "But what has that to do with fish?"

"In those days, when there was little food from the fields, people caught lots of fish and roasted them on the fire."

"I see——" said Arisu.

"So you see why we don't want to explain it in front of dear *Sakana*-chan. Even her name——" the Four of Hearts looked tearful "——even her name comes from the old proverb 'If you can't *suck on a* potato, you can always *suck on a* fish'."

"So fish are called *Sakana*," said Arisu. "*Naruhodo*."

They walked back to the other side of the carriage. All the cards were looking out of the window, pointing things out to *Sakana*-chan. With a sharp creak, the carriage door opened and a rather severe-looking dog in a uniform came in.

He took off his hat and bowed rather peremptorily. "Tickets please," he said.

The cards all presented their tickets.

"What about this odd-looking creature?" asked the conductor. "Do you have a ticket?"

"Oh dear, I'm afraid not," said Arisu.

"That's bad. That's very bad," said the conductor.

"She seems to have a Kanjidex. Couldn't she use an antonym instead?" asked the Four of Hearts.

"I suppose that would be in order," said the conductor. "One antonym, please."

"What's an antonym?" asked Arisu.

"There ought to be one on your Kanjidex," said the conductor. "If there isn't, you'll have to leave the train."

Arisu opened her Kanjidex and saw a button marked *Antonyms*. She tried pressing it.

"Generating antonym..." said the robotic female voice. There were some beeping sounds and then, "Antonym generated."

THE TRAIN OF EVENTS

Two kanji appeared on the Kanjidex screen:

"Will this do?" asked Arisu.
"Not without an explanation," said the conductor.
"We can help with that," said the Four of Hearts.
"That's right," said the Four of Spades. "The first one is used in

atarashii. It means *new*. It contains the Free Radical

which means *axe*."
"Probably it was originally a pick-axe," said the Three of Clubs. "A T-shaped axe under a cliff."
"Because people go mining in the cliffs," said the Two of Hearts.
"So, *stand* in a *tree* with an *axe*—" said Arisu uncertainly.
"Of course, of course!" said the Four of Spades. "You remember *mura*, the village? The first step in making a village is measuring the trees.

"Now once someone gets started on a new village, well, you can imagine them standing in a tree surveying the land with a shiny new axe, ready to get started."

"Pretty soon new things are spouting all over," said the Three of Clubs excitedly. "New timber, new door frames, new cleared land, new fields, new everything."

"And those people, they were enthusiastic," said the Four of Spades. "Everything was new. And they didn't move slowly—they did everything *at a rush*. That's why anything new got called *at-a-rush-y*."

"So what about the other kanji?" asked the conductor.

"It's the antonym of *atarashii*, of course, so it must mean *old*," said the Three of Clubs.

"It is used to make

furui," said the Four of Hearts. "Now imagine that same village years and years later. All the people who built it are old. Many are already in the graveyard. Here is *Kuchi*-chan playing a gravestone with *Juu* as her prop."

"One of my best roles, I think," said *Kuchi* proudly.

"You be quiet," said the conductor. "You're an old gravestone. You're supposed to be as silent as the tomb."

"*Shitsurei*," muttered *Kuchi*.

"So why is it called *furui*?" asked the conductor, who seemed anxious to catch someone out on something.

"Things only get old after everything has come to *furuition*," said the Four of Hearts. "And I think I should mention that *furui* does not mean *old person*, only *old thing*. But that's fine because we are thinking of an old village and its old graveyard. A new village doesn't have a graveyard at all."

"*Furuition*," said the conductor. "I suppose that'll do."

THE TRAIN OF EVENTS

Everyone breathed a sigh of relief.

"*But*," said the conductor. "What about this here fish? Does she have a ticket?"

"She's baggage," said the Four of Spades.

"She *was* baggage," said the conductor. "She was in a bag when she came on. I hung her up *takai* on the 'igh tack. But now she's out of the bag enjoyin' the scenery. That makes her a passenger. She needs a ticket. If she doesn't have a ticket, I'll be obliged to roast her and eat her in lieu of fare."

"You wouldn't do that to dear *Sakana*-chan!" cried the Two of Hearts.

"Oh, wouldn't I? I'm very partial to a nice piece of *Sakana*. You know the old sayin': 'If you can't suck on a—'"

The Two of Hearts started crying.

"Conductor-san, you are showing a remarkable lack of delicacy," said the Four of Hearts.

"I apologize for that and all, ma'am," said the conductor. "But I'm just doin' my job."

"What if we get another antonym?" asked Arisu. "Will that do?"

"I *suppose* it will," said the conductor, looking extremely disappointed.

Arisu opened her Kanjidex again and touched the Antonym button.

"Antonym generated."

"That's a nice easy pair," said the Four of Hearts. "The first one…"

"It's two evenings," interrupted Arisu.

"Two evening moons," said the Four of Hearts. "It means *many*. Easy to remember from the Native American expression *many moons*."

"It looks just like katakana TA, twice," said the Two of Hearts, who had just learned her katakana.

"But when it means evening, it's pronounced *yuu*, not *ta*," said Arisu, who also liked to show off her recently acquired knowledge. "How is it pronounced when it's doubled and means many?"

"When there are two of them it *is* usually pronounced *ta*," said the Four of Spades.

"I guess it took two of them to get the message across," said Arisu.

"Except in the very common word *ooi*," said the Four of Hearts.

"That means *many*," said the Three of Clubs, taking an interest in the conversation. "Take the *ki* out of *ookii*, big, and you get *ooi*, many. You know, when you defeat the big monster in a game—taking its spirit *(ki)* out of it—it sometimes turns into many little monsters."

"I hate it when that happens," said Arisu.

"Just as *ooi*, many, is related to *ookii*, big, so few is related to little," said the Four of Hearts.

"*Shou*, few, not only looks like *shou*, little, with an extra stroke, but her glue-name is the same," said the Four of Spades.

"We can think of a *few* little penguins sliding down the slide," said the Four of Hearts.

"This *shou* also appears in the common word *sukunai:*

THE TRAIN OF EVENTS

which, of course, also means *few*," said the Four of Spades.

"And you can put the two antonyms together like this," said the Three of Clubs excitedly.

"Oh! There are no kana, so I expect they are both using their glue-names. So is it *ta-shou*?" asked Arisu.

"That's right," said the Four of Hearts. "And it means just what you'd expect. More or less, somewhat, a certain amount (not too large or small since they balance each other out)."

The conductor stamped the antonym, bowed and left the carriage.

"*Doumo arigatou gozaimasu*," said the Four of Hearts.

"*Kochira koso, arigatou gozaimasu*," said Arisu. She sat back in her seat and watched the cards enjoy their journey.

As the train rattled on,

Gattan gotton, gattan gotton, gattan gotton...

Arisu found her eyelids becoming heavy.

"I can't be falling asleep," she said to herself. "I *am* asleep, aren't I?"

Gattan gotton, gattan gotton, gattan gotton...

Her eyes closed. She forced herself to open them again, afraid that Kanji Land might disappear. She was still in the carriage, but the playing cards now just looked like a few ordinary playing cards lying on the seats. She picked one up and turned it over. There were three kanji on the back, but she couldn't read them. She only recognized the middle one. It was…

"*Ten*, heaven. What does that mean?" she asked herself aloud.

"That's just the *kaisha*. Where we come from," said the Four of Hearts.

"Oh! I thought you'd gone," said Arisu.

"Oh no. We're still here. It is you who nearly disappeared."

"I did?"

"You did."

Arisu put her hand over her mouth in surprise.

"Ah! Five fingers!" cried the Four of Spades. "Well, that explains it, of course."

"Explains what?" asked Arisu. "And what is the *kaisha*?"

"The *kaisha*, *ne*," said the Four of Hearts gently.

"I know the first one," said Arisu. "It's *meet*. Two selves meeting under one roof. *Au*."

THE TRAIN OF EVENTS

"Yes," said the Four of Hearts. "The glue-name is *kai*. And the other kanji—"

"It's *Tsuchi*, earth, isn't it?" said Arisu. "But I'm not sure about the left-hand part."

"That's a Free Radical," said the Four of Hearts.

"It looks like katakana NE," said Arisu.

"*Ne*, so it does," said the Four of Hearts. "Though what it actually is is an altar."

"An altar," said Arisu. "So that kanji is an earth altar?"

"Yes," said the Four of Hearts. "You remember how a temple measures the earth? This is an altar of the earth. An altar that regards the very land as sacred. A Shinto shrine."

"Really?" said Arisu. "So that word means *meeting at the shrine*."

"Yes," said the Four of Spades. "Long, long ago the shrine was the center of all social life. The heart of the *mura* and the *machi*. When people got together to do anything they would meet at the shrine. That is how the first businesses were formed. The great, great, great-ancestors of the modern Japanese *kaisha* or corporation."

"That must have been a very long time ago," said Arisu. "Was it back when *Kai*, shells, were being used as money?"

"Yes, it was. And the head of the first really big company was called the *Kai-Shah*, the King of Shells, or King of Money."

"So the place you come from—the name I can't read with heaven in the middle—that's a *kaisha*?"

"Yes. The name actually means—" The Four of Spades went into a long explanation of the name and Arisu tried to concentrate, but her eyes closed again. She forced them open and once again the cards looked like ordinary playing cards. There was also a cardboard box with a big Ace of Hearts on the front that must have been the box they came in.

Arisu picked up the box and saw a faded yellow sticker on it with the word

"I wonder what that is," said Arisu. "A *female* in a *house*."

"Oh, don't look at *that*," said the Four of Hearts. Now she seemed properly alive again.

"It's nothing to be ashamed of," said the Four of Spades. "It just says *yasui*. The lady of the house has to practice economy. She has to look for bargains—"

"It means *cheap*," said the Four of Hearts, with tears in her eyes. "That's what it means. It means we were *cheap*."

"We were reduced in price," said the Four of Spades. "Many of the best people get reduced in price, you know."

"We were *yasui* because nobody wanted us," cried the Four of Hearts.

"Not at all," said the Four of Spades. "*Everybody* wanted us, so the kind *kaisha* made us *yasui*, so that everyone could have us. Being *yasui* is something to be proud of. What do you say, children?"

The Three of Clubs and the Two of Hearts started chanting proudly

"*Yasui! Yasui! Yas we* are! *Yasui! Yasui! Yas we* are!"

Somehow their chanting merged with the train's

Gattan gotton, gattan gotton, gattan gotton…

Arisu's eyes closed, her head fell forward, and she fell completely asleep.

20

Was It a Dream?

The train pulled to a halt and Arisu opened her eyes. There were no playing cards in the carriage, not even in the form of ordinary cardboard ones. Perhaps they had gotten out at an earlier station while she was asleep.

She looked out of the window and saw Mr. Hatter running toward the carriage. He had The Doll under one arm.

Mr. Hatter opened the carriage door and gallantly handed Arisu out.

"You came to meet me," said Arisu. "*Arigatou gozaimasu.*"

"*Mainichi, mainichi,*" said Mr. Hatter.

"I beg your pardon?" said Arisu.

"I am afraid I have no pardon, but if I had any I would give it to you freely without any need to beg."

"I meant what did you say?"

"I said *mai-nichi.*"

"Oh, that's *o-Hi-sama* who is sometimes *Nichi.*"

"Yes. It means day in this case. Every day is sun-day in Japan."

"And the other one has *o-kaa-san,* mother."

"Corright. And a Free Radical. It's the on-top version of *hito.*"

"*Hito* and *mother*—"

"Prezactly. It means every. Because *every hito* has a *mother.*"

"And it's said *mai*—"

ALICE IN KANJI LAND

"Of course it is. Because every *hito* calls her mother *mai* mother. Even though it's not *my* mother at all, it's *her* mother. But that's one of the Mysteries of Life. *Every hito* has a mother and *every hito* calls her mother *mai* mother even though the only real *mai* mother is *my* mother."

"So *mai-nichi* means *every day*?"

"Naturally. What else would it mean?"

"And why did you say it?"

"Because I come to meet you at this station every day."

"But you don't."

"Of course I do."

"We only met this morning."

"I know we did. But does that stop us being old friends? I think you are becoming a little repetitive. And we have more important matters on hand."

"What matters?"

Mr. Hatter pointed at The Doll under his arm. "I think she is falling asleep."

"Is that bad?"

"That depends on your point of view, I imagine. But it certainly changes things. Not so much for me as for you."

"How does it change things?"

"Well, look at this." Mr. Hatter drew a large kanji in the air.

"That's a *sphere* made up of the *Monarch* and with the little *Royal Jewel*," said Arisu.

"And surrounded by an all-around Free Radical

WAS IT A DREAM?

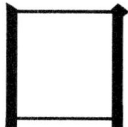

that means boundaries or borders. So it is the whole territory controlled by the Monarch or the Royal Orb. In other words, the country."

"What country?"

"Whatever country it happens to be. In this case, *Kanji no Kuni*—Kanji Land."

"It is said *kuni*?"

"It is."

"Why?"

"Because there are 92 countries in the world."

"92? As many as that? But why... oh, I *see*. *Ku-Ni*."

"Yes. And Kanji Land is the biggest and best of them all."

"So why is it fading out?"

"Ah, that's the point. It isn't fading out for me. It's only fading out for you."

"Why is it fading out for me?" asked Arisu in alarm.

"I told you. Because The Doll is falling asleep."

There was a knocking sound like thunder.

"What's that?" asked Arisu.

"It's for you," said Mr. Hatter.

"For me?"

"Yes, you'd better answer it or it'll get louder."

The thundery knocking came again. Louder, just as Mr. Hatter had said.

"Come in, 'Arry," said Arisu sleepily.

"What's this Harry nonsense?" said her sister.

Arisu half-opened her eyes. "Oh, it's you, *Oneechan*."

"I'm not sure I like *Oneechan* much better than Harry. I'm not Japanese, you know, Alice."

"I can't hear you," said Arisu.

"That's a pity. Then I won't be able to give you your present."

Arisu opened her eyes properly. She was in her own room, lying fully clothed on her bed. Her sister was holding a bag with something quite large in it.

"What present?"

"Call me something better than *Oneechan* and I'll give it to you."

Arisu pressed her palms together and said "*Oneesama*" very reverently.

Her sister burst out laughing. "Here you are then. It's only a book. And it has no pictures or conversations, so I don't know if you'll like it. But it was cheap in the second-hand bookstore and it is about Japanese."

"I'll like it then," said Arisu. "*Arigatou gozaimasu.*"

"*Ari*-what?"

"Thank you, *Oneesama*."

Her sister left the room, and Arisu stood up and looked around her. Had she dreamed it all? Right here? So not only the White Rabbit and Kanji Land were dreams—even the Boring Person and the book had been a dream.

She looked at the chair in the corner. There was The Doll sitting as lifeless as ever. When she was little she used to think The Doll was alive. Maybe that was why The Doll had appeared in the dream.

Arisu didn't want it to be a dream. Maybe it wasn't a dream. Maybe the Kanjidex was still in the pocket of her blue dress. Maybe the little bag of *fun*. There should still be four of them left.

But there was nothing in her pocket except a hard candy and a worn-down yellow pencil.

It *was* a dream.

She opened the bag her sister had given her. Inside was a large book. She looked at the title.

2,136 Joyo Kanji

WAS IT A DREAM?

"How curious," she said to herself. "So that book *does* exist. But I guess I read the title somewhere."

She opened it up and looked at the first few kanji. *Ichi*, *Ni* and *San*. Well, those were pretty obvious. *Yon*. Oh yes, dear funny *Yon*. Arisu remembered how *Ichi* and *San* had made a box around the runaway legs.

And there was *Roku*. "Dear little *Roku*-kun with his nice hat on. That was the first hat I saw in Kanji Land, and goodness, I've seen so *many* now.

"Oh, and there's *Sen*-san. I wonder if he really drinks too much. His hat is still on crooked.

"Oh, oh! There's *Kuruma*-san. She was so kind and friendly when I felt alone."

Then Arisu realized.

"But I know them! I *know* all these kanji. There are hundreds more I don't know, but I know all these ones at the beginning. Dozens of them. I don't just know them, I've *met* them. Even lots I *don't* know, I can recognize the parts that make them up.

"And these are *real* kanji in a real book. I couldn't have learned kanji I didn't know from my own dream, could I?"

Arisu thought it all over very carefully. No matter which way she looked at it the answer was clear.

"*Yatta!*" she shouted. "It *wasn't* a dream!"

She looked through the book some more. There were all her friends and her adventures. Somewhere—*somewhere*, Mimi-sensei was shouting "*Minasan!*" Somewhere, *Shiro* the Sheer White Maiden was rowing people across the moat to the Tower of the Ancients. Somewhere, little *Kuchi*, the Great Actress, was playing hundreds of different roles with dozens of different props. Somewhere *Sakana*-chan was sharing the life of the Card Family from her bowl. Somewhere—

Arisu looked across the room to the chair where The Doll was sitting.

"And that means—"

She picked up The Doll.

"It's all real, isn't it? And so you must be alive. At least sometimes. And somewhere, far away but as near as a dream, Kanji Land really exists.

"Can I get back there? Can *you* help me to get back? There is so much more to learn and I don't want to learn it out of a dusty old book like this."

The Doll said nothing.

Arisu looked at *2,136 Jōyō Kanji*. It was probably a very useful book. And terribly kind of *Oneechan* to buy it for her, even if it was *yasui*. And Arisu would *ganbaru* with it, she promised herself.

But—but kanji weren't dead things in textbooks. They were alive and dancing. Living, breathing realities, full of joy and sorrow, kindness and craziness. Arisu knew that now.

"You *will* take me back there some day, won't you?" she said rather plaintively to The Doll.

But The Doll was sound asleep.

Afterword

How to Use the *Alice in Kanji Land* SRS Deck

The *Alice in Kanji Land* SRS Deck is designed to cement the kanji, words and pronunciations (with audio) learned in this book into your long-term memory. It is available at no cost. The deck can be downloaded from http://learnjapaneseonline.info/alice-deck/ See the instructions below.

About SRS

SRS (Spaced Repetition Software) works like conventional flash cards, only instead of being random, it exposes you to the cards at ever-lengthening intervals based on the way human memory works. So, essentially, it re-introduces a card a little *before* the time you would naturally be forgetting it, so that you strengthen your long-term memory of it.

If you successfully remember it, the next interval will be longer. However, the system also adapts to your memory and the particular words you personally find easier or more difficult. The whole thing is based on algorithms that replicate the way human memory works and passes knowledge from short-term to long-term memory.

About the *Alice in Kanji Land* Deck

The *Alice in Kanji Land Deck* is based on the idea that you will read one chapter of this book per day and use the deck every day (starting with Chapter 2).

If you get involved in the story and want to read ahead, that's fine. If you want to read the whole book in advance, that's fine too. The more you look at the stories and the information contained in them the better. But to use the deck you should make one chapter per day your focus-chapter.

Since the deck and your reading won't sync exactly, it is best to keep your focused reading a little bit ahead of the deck.

The cards all give chapter numbers and reminders of the relevant story incidents. If you find you have forgotten a word and the information on the card is insufficient, go back to the chapter and remind yourself of that part of the story. Note that the book's Table of Contents also lists the kanji introduced in each chapter, in order of appearance.

You don't need to know all the information on the back of a card. Just the word's *meaning* and *pronunciation*. The other notes are just there to help you if you forget something. Use them as much or little as you need.

And remember that this is *your* deck. You are free to personalize it if you want to. If you find yourself constantly forgetting a particular kanji or confusing two kanji, you can write a little reminder-note on the *back* (not the front—this is important) of the card to clarify things for yourself. Just hit the *Edit* button on the bottom left of the card.

You can even drag pictures onto the back of the card if you want to!

If the deck is introducing new cards too fast or too slow for you, go to *Options* → *New Cards* and change the *New cards/day* number up or down. If you want to slow down the pace or power through the deck, be my guest.

If you already know some of the kanji/words so well that you are *sure* you don't need them in the deck, just go ahead and delete the cards (Anki calls them *notes*). No point wasting review time on things you really don't need. You can also *suspend* a card if you want to stop reviewing it but think you might possibly want it back some time. You do both these things from Anki's *Browse* screen or from the top-right drop-down menu on your mobile device.

If any of this sounds confusing, don't worry. The deck will work fine right out of the box. You don't *need* to do anything except review it.

Please keep up reviews even after you have finished the book. At a normal pace it shouldn't take more than 15 minutes even on the biggest days (they do vary) and as the deck stops introducing new cards, the review time will gradually diminish to very little.

About Anki

Anki is a free SRS system and probably the best and most sophisticated available at any price. It can be downloaded at no cost for Windows, Macintosh, Linux, Amazon Kindle and Android devices (the Android/Kindle version is called AnkiDroid). The iOS (iPhone/iPad) version is not free, presumably on the theory that iOS owners are rich and developers need to eat. The second proposition is undoubtedly true.

You can also set up a free AnkiWeb account and sync your deck and its current progress, together with any changes you make to it, across your devices.

You need to install Anki on your device, download the *Alice in Kanji Land Deck* (http://learnjapaneseonline.info/alice-deck) and open it in your Anki. In most cases you can just double-click the *Alice in Kanji Land Deck* file from your desktop to open it automatically in Anki. On future occasions you can just open Anki and it will be there.

Please note that the *Alice in Kanji Land Deck* should come as one .apkg file. If your computer tries to unpack it into a folder of sub-files (mostly only a problem with a few older Macs) please ignore the unpacked version and use the original file you downloaded.

Kanji as Words

The Alice Method is not about learning kanji "in the raw". Kanji in the deck come as words, and the pronunciation of each word is reinforced by an audio recording on the back of the card that plays automatically (unless you turn it off or turn your sound down). The pronunciation is also shown in hiragana, so you don't need to have the sound on.

If a kanji does not make a word on its own, one or more of its most basic word-forms will be in the deck. Two- and three-kanji words from the book are also included in the deck so that you can get used to on-readings ("glue-names") and how words fit together.

How to Review

This will be largely obvious as you actually use it.

1. Open Anki

2. Click the *Alice in Kanji Land Deck* from Anki's start screen.
   (It may ask if you want to study. If so, say yes.)

3. Look at the kanji or word presented to you. Decide what it means and how it is said. Click *Show Answer*. (Or you can just hit the spacebar or swipe the screen of your mobile device.)

4. The answer screen is the "back" of the card. It shows you the meaning and pronunciation and also reads the pronunciation aloud. The extra notes give extra information and relevant passages from the story. This is useful if you have forgotten something.
   It gives you *four options* (less on a first-time card).

   A. If you didn't remember correctly, hit the first button (Again or Fail). The card will return for another try in a very short time.

   B. If you got it mostly right but found it difficult, hit the second button (Hard). This will bring the card back more quickly than normal.

   C. This is the one you will be using most of the time and is the default if you simply hit the spacebar or swipe the screen of your mobile device. If you got the card right, hit the third button

HOW TO USE THE ALICE DECK

(Good). This will keep the card coming back at lengthening intervals based on how human memory works.

D. If the card was really easy, hit the fourth button (Easy). This will lengthen the time before the next review of the card. If you hit Easy on the same card a few times, it will start receding further and further into the future but it will still come back occasionally in case you should forget it.

5. Once you have selected your option for the card, the next card will appear. This continues until you have completed your reviews for the day.

And that's it. Most of this will be obvious just by following the on-screen interface.

Note on Meanings and Definitions

If you look at dictionary definitions for some of the simpler words, they are very complex. This is necessary since, for example, someone reading a book will want to know what the word might mean in context.

However, on the cards these are cut down to the most basic meanings. To take a relatively uncomplicated example, the dictionary defines

ue as:

> *above; up; over; elder (e.g. daughter); top; summit; surface; on; before; previous; superiority; one's superior (i.e. one's elder); on top of that; besides; what's more*

In the deck, the card simply gives the definitions *above*, *up* and *over*.

These are the basic meanings of the word, and all the others are derivative of those concepts. The *before* meaning, for example, means higher up the page in a written text. The *on top of that* meaning is exactly the same metaphor as in English.

The best way to learn is to get the basic meaning firmly fixed, rather than try to memorize a sprawling and apparently chaotic list of meanings from the beginning. A little later, you will start to see how the extended and metaphorical meanings derive naturally from the basic meaning.

Professor Isseki's Geeky Notes

Ah, Reader-sama. Good afternoon. Isseki here. You'll find me in Chapter 15 if you don't know who I am.

You don't need to read this section unless you are a bit beyond the beginner stage or you happen to be interested in what the single-figure numbers rather vulgarly refer to as "geeky stuff".

As you may have noticed, *Alice in Kanji Land* is a book about kanji. However, a number of other points of interest arise in the course of the story. Many of them have been dealt with at length by that strange Doll and her friends at KawaJapa.

As I read their papers from time to time (eccentric people but reasonable scholars—for inanimate objects), I thought I would provide a few notes for those who may happen to be interested.

Left and Right (Chapter 5)

Migi and *Hidari* are arguing as usual, about their kanji and everything else. The explanations they offer represent biased scholarship at its worst. For a more serious discussion of the possible historical reasons behind the *migi* and *hidari* kanji, you might care to look at:

http://tinyurl.com/migi-hidari

Leaving or Throwing Out? (Chapter 6)

Deru, as the chapter explains, means *leave*. But we can also say *Dasu* using the same kanji.

What's the difference? *Deru* means *leave* or *come* out. *Dasu* means *take* out or *put* out. In English these are called the *intransitive* and *transitive* versions. In Japanese they are much more sensibly called the *self-move word* and the *other-move word*. Lots of words (such as *hairu/ireru* in the same chapter and *tomaru/tomeru* in the next one) have self-move (go in, stop) and other-move (put in, stop something) versions.

Fortunately, these different versions correspond mostly to a few very simple rules. But sadly they aren't usually taught.

For beginners I do not recommend troubling with all this right now, but if you are a little more advanced you may want to go here:

http://tinyurl.com/self-move

This paper tells you how to find your way with relative ease through what usually seems like a maze of transitive and intransitive verbs. For example, you will learn how *deru/dasu* and *tomaru/tomeru* are completely predictable, because the *-su* and *-meru* versions of any pair are *always* transitive.

Sound Sisters (Chapter 18)

Very few people seem to know about the Sound Sisters, which is unfortunate because they make a great deal of kanji pronunciation much easier.

You will find a full introduction to the Sisters here:

http://tinyurl.com/sound-sisters

There is even a free Anki deck to help you learn them. Again not something beginners should worry about but very helpful once you become a little more advanced.

Glossary of Japanese Words Used by Characters in the Book

The characters in Kanji Land speak a language closer to Japanese than English, but one that Arisu can mysteriously understand. For the purposes of this book, it is rendered mostly as English but with a little Japanese that readers may understand to help convey something of the flavor of what is being said.

I have tried to restrict those little bits of Japanese to words and phrases known to most people who have some interest in the language without having studied it seriously. However, since most beginners know a few things one doesn't expect and don't know a few things one does expect, here is a brief guide to those words and phrases not introduced in the kanji explanations or otherwise explained in the story. Plus a very few notes on English usage.

The words are listed roughly in order of appearance in the story.

Follow That Rabbit

Ganbaru: "Try hard, do one's best".

Yo: Emphasizer; marker for information not known to listener.

BE~DA: "Nyah!" Childish rude exclamation that is usually accompanied by the rude gesture described in the text (which is known as *akanbe*).

(O)jou: Polite way to address a girl; can be used with any of the following three honorific suffixes, which modify the tone of *o-jou*.

> *Chan:* Cute suffix, not especially respectful; can be affectionate or may just emphasize that the person addressed is young.
>
> *San:* Normal honorific.
>
> *Sama:* Very respectful honorific.

Osoku narimashita: "(I) became (and therefore am) late".

Usagi: "Rabbit".

Sumimasen: "(I'm) sorry" or "Excuse me"; sometimes also "Thank you".

Hon: "Book" (see Chapter 10 for the kanji).
Dame: As used here, "no-no, not allowed".
Sakura: "Cherry blossom".

Itchy-Knee-San Is a Japanese Count

Oniichan: Familiar term for one's own elder brother.
Atashi: Feminine form of *watashi*—"I".
Hajimemashite: Cultural equivalent of "pleased to meet you".
Yoroshiku onegaishimasu: Literally something like "Please be good to me". Said on first meeting. Less formal variants are a simple *yoroshiku*, *yoroshiku ne* etc. The proper reply is also *yoroshiku (onegaishimasu)*.
Eeto: Hesitation-word like "er".
Doko: "Where".
Sou desu ka: "Is that so?"
Hai: "Yes" (formal/respectful).
Gomen nasai: Polite form of "Forgive (me)"; often a child's form of apology.

The Rad Hatter

Kun: Honorific used for boys.
Kochira koso: Literally something like "this side especially", often meaning "It is I who should be saying…" when returning a greeting.

The Tower of the Ancients

Sonna koto: Literally "Such a thing"; a phrase modestly used to deflect praise, implying "such a thing is not the case".
Chibi: "Small (person)"; can be affectionate or disparaging.
Haitte: Te-form of *hairu*, enter (see Chapter 6); short for a phrase such as *haitte kudasai*, therefore meaning "(please) come in".

The Middle Way

Eigo wa baka ne: "English is silly, isn't it?"
Pin-pon: Sound made in Japanese quiz shows for a right answer.
Sore de wa: Common phrase meaning something like "Now then".

GLOSSARY OF JAPANESE WORDS

Kin-Kon-KAN-Kon

Kin-kon-kan-kon: Japanese school chime used in most schools. It is the Westminster Chime, based on the chime of Big Ben, the bell of Elizabeth Tower at the Palace of Westminster, London.

Naruhodo: "I see (now I understand)".

Sensei: "Teacher".

Gaya-Gaya: Murmuring or chattering of a group of people.

Minasan: Minna is "everybody" but when an honorific is appended it loses its first *n* sound.

Shizuka ni: Literally, "quietly" (adverbial form of *shizuka na*); short for *shizuka ni suru*—literally, "do quietly" or better "act quietly", thus "be quiet". Similar truncated forms are used in English, such as "Quiet, please" for "Be quiet, please".

Down by the Riverside

Yoku ganbatta: "(You) tried hard, worked well".

The Car that Drove Herself

Daijoubu: "All right, okay"; here short for "Are you all right?"

Tadaima: This is what Japanese people say when they return home. Literally "just now": *tada*=just, *ima*=now. It is short for *tada ima kaerimashita*—"I have just now returned".

The Man Behind the Hats

Ohayou gozaimasu: Cultural equivalent of "good morning". Literally, a very polite way of saying "It is early"; more informally, just *ohayou*.

The Time Machine

Mata ne: Equivalent to "I'll see you later".

Relativity

Tarinai: "Insufficient".

Inside the Treasure Cave

Kara: "From" or as here, "Because", coming after rather than before the explanation.

The Road to Nowhere

Namaiki na: The White Rabbit is talking to himself (indicated by *na*) about Arisu's being impudent.

Ano, sumimasen: Ano is a hesitation word. Taken together, the phrase is a polite calling of someone's attention, like "excuse me".

Irasshaimase: Used in shops to welcome customers.

No-Tea with the Baron

Tuxedo: What the Baron was actually wearing was morning dress, but since this might give a false or confusing impression, I used the slightly inaccurate term tuxedo (which means dinner jacket, though it is sometimes used to include more formal evening dress).

Silk hat: I have used both terms, silk hat and top hat, in the book for the hats made by Mr. Hatter. Top hat is more familiar and conjures up the correct hat. Silk hat is older and more formal, especially appropriate for the Baron. Japanese uses both terms: katakana SHIRUKU HATTO and TOPPU HATTO.

The Train of Events

Shitsurei: "Rude"; literally "lacking politeness".

Arigatou gozaimasu: "Thank you"; adding *doumo* intensifies it to the level of "Thank you very much".

Was It a Dream?

Oneechan: Familiar term for one's own elder sister; cf. *Oniichan*.

Oneesama: Reverential term for an elder sister.

Also by Cure Dolly

Unlocking Japanese

A ground-breaking book that sets out to demonstrate that Japanese is "simple, logical and beautiful" and that most of the apparently "arbitrary rules" that you "just have to learn" can be reduced to simple, easily intuitive patterns if you just understand how the language really works.

An Alien Doll in Japan

A unique look at Japan, covering the Doll's first month in Aichi Prefecture. At the time of going to Japan, Cure Dolly had been learning Japanese for about a year, using the self-immersion methods she advocates. She put her theories into practice by adopting the challenge of using no language other than Japanese during the whole of her stay, even in emergencies (of which there were several).

KawaJapa

Cure Dolly founded and writes for the KawaJapa website and has a related channel on YouTube (KawaJapa CureDolly Channel).

Printed in Great Britain
by Amazon